TITLE: HEY GOD, CAN WE TALK? DEVOTIONAL WORKBOOK JOURNAL

COPYRIGHT © 2024
THE MARRIAGE LAB LLC.
COPYRIGHT NOTICE: BY MRS. TAMIKA BOWE-LACROIX. ALL RIGHT RESERVED.
ISBN: 978-0-9992408-3-0
THE ABOVE INFORMATION FORMS THIS COPYRIGHT NOTICE: © 2024 BY TAMIKA BOWE. ALL RIGHTS RESERVED.
EDITED BY: DAWN SULLIVAN
THIS BOOK, OR PARTS THEREOF, MAY NOT BE REPRODUCED
IN ANY FORM WITHOUT PERMISSION, EXCEPT IN CASE OF BRIEF QUOTATIONS.
CONTACT **INFO@YOURMARRIAGELAB.COM**
ALL RIGHTS RESERVED.
ALL SCRIPTURE QUOTATIONS ARE TAKEN FROM THE HOLY BIBLE, NEW INTERNATIONAL VERSION® (NIV®). COPYRIGHT © 1973, 1978, 1984, 2011 BY BIBLICA, INC.™ USED BY PERMISSION. ALL RIGHTS RESERVED WORLDWIDE.
THIS BOOK IS LICENSED FOR YOUR PERSONAL ENJOYMENT ONLY AND NOT TO SERVE AS ANY MEDICAL ADVICE OR TREATMENT. ALWAYS CONSULT YOUR PHYSICIAN FOR GUIDANCE BEFORE ALTERING OR CHANGING ANY MEDICATION. NO PART OF THIS BOOK MAY BE REPRODUCED OR TRANSMITTED IN ANY FORM OR BY ANY MEANS, ELECTRONIC OR MECHANICAL, INCLUDING PHOTOCOPYING, RECORDING OR BY ANY INFORMATION STORAGE AND RETRIEVAL SYSTEM, WITHOUT WRITTEN PERMISSION FROM THE AUTHOR.
THANK YOU FOR RESPECTING
THE PROPRIETARY WORK OF THE AUTHOR.

WORKBOOK JOURNAL

this book belongs to:

_____

Acknowledgements

I am grateful for my family. My husband, my kids, my parents, my sister, and my friends—you have all played such a vital role in contributing to the completion of this devotional. I wouldn't have been able to do this without you. Your unwavering encouragement and belief in me have pushed me to reach levels I didn't think I was capable of achieving.

To my husband James, thank you for being my rock and my greatest cheerleader. Your love, patience, and constant reassurance reminded me to keep going, even when the process felt overwhelming.

To my kids; Jourdan, Julien and Jameson, you inspire me every day to be the best version of myself. Your joy, faith, and unconditional love have been a source of light in this journey.

To my parents Nana and Papi, thank you for the foundation of faith and love you instilled in me. Your prayers, wisdom, and support have been a lifeline during this process.

To my sister Dawn, thank you for being my confidant and sounding board. Your words of encouragement and thoughtful advice kept me grounded and motivated to see this project through to the end.

Chosen Wives Ministries; Trishon, Bianca, Nadia, Turkessa, Lakia, and Lacretia, words can hardly capture how profoundly this ministry has impacted my life, but I'll do my best to express it. When I hear people talk about how hard it is for women to find true friendship, I realize how blessed I am because of all of you. You women have shown me what real, authentic friendship looks like. I thank God daily for this ministry because it's the kind of connection so many dream of having—a sisterhood built on prayer, encouragement, and love. Here, there's no room for gossip, only genuine support. You are women who walk through life together, weathering storms, fighting spiritual battles, and interceding for one another. You have no idea how invaluable this ministry has been to me. Your transparency, authenticity, and willingness to stand in prayer with me every day have been a cornerstone of my healing, growth, and transformation. Thank you for being part of my journey and for reminding me of the power of God-centered friendship.

To Win Women Empower, I've only been here for a short while but you don't have to be in the community long to realize how powerful you women are. Your testimonies are like no other. You women have carried burdens that many wouldn't make it through. In spite of, you all carry the peace of God. You ladies are the exact demonstration of Gods love! Thank you for your vulnerability. Thank you for being authentic. I had many of you in mind when I created this devotional because regardless of what you have been through, you show up for others. It takes strength and courage to be who God has called you to be so I thank you for your faithfulness.

This devotional is a reflection of the love and support I've received from my communities. Thank you for your patience with me throughout this process, for understanding the late nights and moments of stress, and for always lifting me up. I dedicate this work to you.

THE TWELVE STEPS

1 Hey God, Am I Enough? — 15
2 Hey God, Help me to acknowledge my pain. — 33
3 Hey God, Help me to see me as your image. — 53
4 Hey God, Fix me where I am broken. — 72
5 Hey God, is pleasure my birthright? — 92
6 Hey God, Help me to overcome my limited beliefs. — 112
7 Hey God, Help me to understand and pursue purpose. — 132
8 Hey God, Help me to trust the process. — 155
9 Hey God, Help me to stay aligned with my goals. — 173
10 Hey God, Help me to create habits for success. — 192
11 Hey God, Help me with accountability. — 210
12 Hey God, I am Empowered! — 228
13 Bonus: Walking Boldly in Your Transformation. — 240

"Hey God, Can We Talk?"

WELCOME

Hey Saints!

As an intimacy coach, my primary mission is to assist individuals in cultivating a deeper and more profound connection with their spirituality to understand how they fit into the equation with God. This means creating a space that allows them to be vulnerable enough to engage in meaningful conversations with God.

Hey God, Can We Talk?, is an actionable workbook devotional designed to provide you with the structure and tools required to deepen that spiritual connection over the course of twelve weeks. It's more than just a guide; it serves as a structured path to a meaningful and personal relationship with yourself and God. As you go through this healing process, you need to be moving in a direction that produces growth. The goal is that you will learn a little more about who you are by applying actionable steps in the process of transformation so that growth will happen.

By the end of twelve weeks, you'll have fostered a profound connection with God and be the version of yourself you deserve to know. You're on a transformative path of self-discovery and spiritual growth that focuses on key areas of your life and *'Hey God, Can We Talk?'* is here to guide you towards that.

May it inspire and support you in deepening your connection and becoming the version of yourself that you didn't know existed. Welcome to the journey!

ABOUT ME

Tammy LaCroix

I am Tammy, the Biblical sexuality queen and your favorite intimacy and relationship coach. I love what I do which is why I created, **The Marriage Lab LLC.** The lab offers a curated range of faith-based intimacy products that enhance emotional and physical connection. In the lab, you'll find spiritual tools and resources to help couples build a God-centered marriage, and help women to become whole before marriage.

You can find us on our, *'Sex for Saints'* podcasts, selling books, speaking engagements, and facilitating workshops, bridging the gap between faith and intimacy. We provide practical guidance and inspiration for couples to strengthen their bond and live out God's design for marriage.

HOW TO USE THIS BOOK!

How to Use This Book: A 12-Week Journey of Transformation

This devotional is designed to guide you on a 12-week journey of self-discovery, healing, and empowerment. Each week focuses on a specific area of growth, allowing you to reflect, pray, and take actionable steps toward personal and spiritual transformation.

Here's how to get the most out of this book:

- **Commit to the Process** - Set aside dedicated time each day or week to read, reflect, and apply the lessons. Transformation takes intentionality, so approach this journey with an open heart and a willingness to grow.
- **Engage with the Content** - Each chapter contains reflections, prayers, and exercises designed to help you dig deeper. Don't rush—take the time to meditate on each topic and journal your thoughts as God speaks to your heart.
- **Apply What You Learn** - End each week with practical steps to integrate the lessons into your life. Growth happens when you move beyond reading to action.
- **Stay Accountable** - Consider inviting a friend, mentor, or small group to join you on this journey. Sharing insights and experiences will deepen your growth and keep you accountable.

Additional Tips for Success:

- **Journal Your Journey**: Use a journal to capture your reflections, prayers, and actions each week.
- **Pray and Meditate Daily**: Begin and end each week with prayer, inviting God to guide your growth.
- **Celebrate Small Wins**: Recognize and celebrate your progress along the way.
- **Be open and honest with yourself.** This journal is a personal space for you to explore your spirituality and connect with God.
- **Do not rush the process**. Take your time with each step and savor your conversations with God. If a chapter takes you longer than a week, that is okay. Remember this is your journey so do what you need to do to ensure you get all that you need.
- **Join the FACEBOOK group.** You need support and accountability for your journey. the group is a safe space with like minded individuals who want to talk to God together. **FB: Hey God, Can We Talk?**

By following this 12-week plan, you'll embark on a transformational journey that leads to healing, purpose, and empowerment. Let this devotional be your guide as you step into the fullness of who God has created you to be!

Step
workbook
one

Hey God, Am I Enough?

Begin your journey by addressing feelings of inadequacy. Reflect on your identity in Christ and affirm your worth as a child of God.

This Month, I Declare That:

DECLARATIONS

1. The Lord is my shepherd, and I lack nothing (Psalm 23:1).
2. No weapon formed against me will prosper, and I will refute every tongue that accuses me (Isaiah 54:17).
3. The joy of the Lord is my strength, and I will rejoice in Him daily (Nehemiah 8:10).
4. God's plans for me are good, and He will give me hope and a future (Jeremiah 29:11).
5. I am fearfully and wonderfully made, and I will walk confidently in my identity (Psalm 139:14).
6. God will work all things together for my good because I love Him (Romans 8:28).
7. I am the head and not the tail; I will walk in favor and abundance (Deuteronomy 28:13).
8. I will meditate on God's Word day and night, and it will bring me success (Joshua 1:8).
9. The Lord will go before me and make my crooked paths straight (Isaiah 45:2).
10. I will abide in Christ, and my life will bear much fruit for His glory (John 15:5).
11. God's peace, which surpasses all understanding, will guard my heart and mind (Philippians 4:7).
12. The Lord is my light and salvation; I will not fear anything or anyone (Psalm 27:1).
13. I will be strong and courageous, for the Lord is with me wherever I go (Joshua 1:9).
14. I am seated in heavenly places with Christ, and I walk in spiritual authority (Ephesians 2:6).
15. I will run and not grow weary; I will walk and not faint, for the Lord renews my strength (Isaiah 40:31).

Goals

This month, I walk in faith, love, victory, and purpose, fully trusting in God's promises! ✨🙏

LET'S CHECK IN

DATE _____

TOP 3 THINGS I WAS INTENTIONAL ABOUT
- _____
- _____
- _____

THIS WEEK I FELT?

WHAT WERE MY PATTERNS?

WHAT DO I NEED TO FOCUS ON NEXT?
_____
_____
_____
_____

WAS I TRIGGERED?

IN WHAT WAY WILL I SHOW UP FOR ME?

MY RANKING OF THE WEEK
★ ★ ★ ★ ★

LET'S CREATE A PLAN

MONDAY | TUESDAY | WEDNESDAY

THURSDAY | FRIDAY | SATURDAY

APPOINTMENT TIMES | SUNDAY | TASK/REMINDERS

KEEP GOING!

Misc. doodle

TO-DO'S

PHOTO/reminders?

Just living my best life.

~ STEP 1 ~

AWARENESS: AM I ENOUGH?

Affirm - "I AM ENOUGH!"

> **Colossians 1:21-23 NIV**
> "Once you were alienated from God and were enemies in your minds because of your evil behavior. But now he has reconciled you by Christ's physical body through death to present you holy in his sight, without blemish and free from accusation if you continue in your faith, established and firm, and do not move from the hope held out in the gospel."

There was a time in my life when I thought very little of myself. Abuse was introduced to my story at the tender age of eight, and for a while, it never ended. As I became older, I found myself in situations that were even more traumatic. Combined with everything else that was going on in my life during that time, it changed something in me… my heart! Because my heart changed, my behavior changed. I began to indulge in sin because I believed it was my option for escape. I lost faith in myself and people. Drinking, partying, and drugs became not just my norm, but my way of escape. Sex was my outlet. Because I was broken, the decisions I made in relationships came from a broken place. I felt unworthy of finding love or that love would find me. My relationships were toxic because I settled, and accepted that as my norm. Not thinking I deserved anything better than what I got made me question, "Was I enough!"

During those periods of my life where I alienated myself from God, not just in my actions, but also in my thought process; my behavior was a result of everything I thought about myself. The destructed actions I did I believed! I didn't believe that something as simple as reading a Bible could change me. I did believe that drinking would take me away from my problems. I believed that if I got high I wouldn't have to think about the things I was going through. I believed that sex was a stress reliever and I was always under a lot of stress! I believed that being surrounded by people meant that I wouldn't feel lonely, but when no one was around I was the loneliest I could ever be. I would pray but I didn't really believe that prayer could change my situations. I would acknowledge God but didn't believe I needed to follow His word.

You are Enough!

I convinced myself that I was not worth more than the life I was living, but I was all wrong! I was in the wrong places and the wrong mindset and I fought hard to stay where I was until God rescued me. God's grace and mercy would be a constant reminder that I was absolutely enough.

God became the bridge in between my actions and what I was feeling to bring me back to Him. I find it interesting that no matter how deep or far gone I thought I was, as a remedy to save me, God offered to me, Himself. He sent His son to be broken, to save me and you because you are enough!

Isn't it amazing that regardless of your choices, good or bad, God finds you worthy enough! He has reconciled you by Christ's physical body through death to present you holy in His sight. Jesus died on a cross as a symbol to show you through His death, to heal you from all of your past trauma, and the things you have experienced. This reconciliation is not just a repaired relationship; it changes your very standing before God. Through Christ, as a believer, you are seen as "holy," "without blemish," and "free from accusation." This means that in God's eyes, you are cleansed, forgiven, and made pure, with no charges held against you because of Jesus' sacrifice. God paid a price for you with His life because you are the most valued being on this earth! I said all of that to say, God paid a price because you are worth it and that makes you enough! How powerful is that?!

Today, I want you to just identify where you are. Are you unhealed, angry, bitter, confused, lost, alone, traumatized, or walking with unforgiveness? Take a moment and talk to God about how you feel in this very moment and declare that because Christ died, you are made new and that makes you enough!

Prayer:

Hey God, my life up to this point has not been easy. Sometimes I don't even know how or what to feel. I sometimes feel lost, confused, and like no one truly understands me, but You do. Thank you for showing me that there is purpose in my life. I might not fully understand why I had to experience some things, but You are teaching me that all things will work out for my good. You find me worthy. You find me cherished. You find me valuable. I know that there is a plan that is bigger for my life even though I sometimes can't fully see it. I am ready to accept where I am so that I can give it all to You. I surrender my life to You, and say have Your way in me! Thank you for freeing me. Thank you for seeing me. Thank you for giving me hope again. In Jesus name I pray. Amen

You are God's Masterpiece!

1. Materials: Grab 10 post-its.
2. On each post-it, write a biblical affirmation - examples are below.
3. Stick them around your house, on your walls or mirror so you can see it daily.
4. Create a morning routine that repeat affirmations out loud everyday for the duration of the 12 weeks.

Examples: Here are 10 affirmations that you can use or find your own.

1. **I am fearfully and wonderfully made** – "I praise You because I am fearfully and wonderfully made; Your works are wonderful, I know that full well." (Psalm 139:14)
2. **I am loved deeply by God** – "For I am convinced that neither death nor life... nor anything else in all creation, will be able to separate us from the love of God." (Romans 8:38-39)
3. **I am chosen and cherished** – "But you are a chosen people, a royal priesthood, a holy nation, God's special possession. (1 Peter 2:9)
4. **God has a purpose and plan for my life** – "For I know the plans I have for you... plans to prosper you and not to harm you, plans to give you hope and a future." (Jeremiah 29:11)
5. **I am strong in Christ** – "I can do all things through Christ who strengthens me." (Philippians 4:13)
6. **I am valuable and treasured** – "Are not five sparrows sold for two pennies? Yet not one of them is forgotten by God... You are worth more than many sparrows." (Luke 12:6-7)
7. **I am God's masterpiece, created for good** – "For we are God's handiwork, created in Christ Jesus to do good works, which God prepared in advance for us to do." (Ephesians 2:10)
8. **God gives me peace and confidence** – "The Lord is my light and my salvation—whom shall I fear? The Lord is the stronghold of my life—of whom shall I be afraid?" (Psalm 27:1)
9. **God is with me, and I am never alone** – "Be strong and courageous... for the Lord your God goes with you; He will never leave you nor forsake you." (Deuteronomy 31:6)
10. **I am a new creation in Christ** – "Therefore, if anyone is in Christ, the new creation has come: The old has gone, the new is here!" (2 Corinthians 5:17)

My Take-away's

1.
2.
3.
4.
5.

DEVOTIONAL NOTES

_____

_____

_____

_____

Top Three Affirmations

★ _____
★ _____
★ _____

Define your goals

▶ _____
▶ _____
▶ _____
▶ _____
▶ _____
▶ _____
▶ _____
▶ _____
▶ _____
▶ _____
▶ _____
▶ _____
▶ _____

Self Care Plans ✅ ❌

1. _____
2. _____
3. _____
4. _____
5. _____
6. _____

Prayer Focus ✅ ❌

1. _____
2. _____
3. _____
4. _____
5. _____
6. _____

Notes

BRAIN DUMP

DATE / /

Hey God, I'm busy a lot! Help me to be intentional.

CLEAR YOUR MIND!
What are all the things I can't stop thinking about?

-
-
-
-
-
-

HIGH PRIORITY
These are my non-negotiables, they have to get done!

-
-
-

LOW PRIORITY
These are important, but can wait.

-
-
-

FREE THOUGHTS
Remember to give yourself grace! You can't be everything to everyone. Fill up your cup and pour from the overflow.

5 Minutes of Meditation

S M T W TH F S

Breathe before writing

INHALE EXHALE INHALE EXHALE INHALE EXHALE

I'm intentionally meditating on?

* _____
* _____
* _____
* _____
* _____

Describe your feelings. You can draw or write.

My Action Step:
_____
_____

Expose meditation lies!

Sometimes, we think about things that are not true. Write down a truth to a lie you heard while meditating and confirm it with a scripture.

Example: I expose the lie that I'm not good enough because God says that I am fearfully and wonderfully made.

This Week's Highlight

Things that you overcame:
_____
_____
_____
_____

"But his delight is in the law of the Lord; and in his law doth he meditate day and night." Psalm 1:2 KJV

Your mind should be clear. It's time to focus and just write.

Hey God, Can We Talk?   Date:

Your mind should be clear. It's time to focus and just write.

Hey God, Can We Talk?   Date:

Your mind should be clear. It's time to focus and just write.

Hey God, Can We Talk?   Date:

Your mind should be clear. It's time to focus and just write.

Hey God, Can We Talk?   Date:

Your mind should be clear. It's time to focus and just write.

Hey God, Can We Talk?   Date:

_____
_____
_____
_____
_____
_____
_____
_____
_____
_____
_____
_____
_____
_____
_____
_____
_____
_____
_____
_____
_____
_____

THE SCRIPTURE THAT KEPT ME ▶

WHAT CAN I DO DIFFERENTLY NEXT TIME?

▶

▶

▶

HOW CAN I REWARD MYSELF?

▶

▶

▶

WHAT WERE MY CHALLENGES? WAS I HARD ON MYSELF? DID I GIVE MYSELF GRACE? HAVE I FORGIVEN MYSELF? LET'S TALK TO GOD ABOUT IT!

I AM ENOUGH MAZE

"I don't know if I am worth it!"

1 John 3:1 NIV
"See what great love the Father has lavished on us, that we should be called children of God! And that is what we are!"

Find the road that leads to, "I Am Enough!"

"I am absolutely worth it!"

"But you are a chosen people, a royal priesthood, a holy nation, God's special possession."(1 Peter 2:9) NIV

Step workbook TWO

Hey God, help me to acknowledge my pain.

Take time to confront and process past hurts. Allow God to meet you in your pain and begin the healing process.

LET'S CHECK IN

DATE _____

TOP 3 THINGS I WAS INTENTIONAL ABOUT
- _____
- _____
- _____

THIS WEEK I FELT?

WHAT WERE MY PATTERNS?

WHAT DO I NEED TO FOCUS ON NEXT?
_____
_____
_____
_____

WAS I TRIGGERED?

IN WHAT WAY WILL I SHOW UP FOR ME?

MY RANKING OF THE WEEK
☆ ☆ ☆ ☆ ☆

LET'S CREATE A PLAN

MONDAY | TUESDAY | WEDNESDAY

THURSDAY | FRIDAY | SATURDAY

APPOINTMENT TIMES | SUNDAY | TASK/REMINDERS

KEEP GOING!

Misc. doodle

TO-DO'S

PHOTO/reminders?

Just living my best life.

~ STEP 2 ~

HEY GOD, HELP ME TO ACKNOWLEDGE THE PAIN.

Affirm - "There is no pain too great for God to heal!"

Psalms 147:3 NIV
"He heals the brokenhearted and binds up their wounds."

I remember being such an outgoing child without a care in this world. The innocence that I carried was taken away the very moment someone decided to inappropriately put their hands on me. My life became a never-ending story of unacknowledged pain after that. The trauma that I experienced showed up in all areas of my life; my family, my relationships, my friendships, my health, and even work. What I didn't realize was that the decisions I made were a result of my pains. I created expectations that were impossible for others to fulfill because my ideologies were birthed from my experiences.

Here are examples of what it looked like for me;

- **In Family:** Isolation, seclusion, resentment, disconnected, misunderstood - (Inability to create boundaries or communicate my needs or ask for help)
- **In Relationships**: Fear of intimacy, hypervigilance - sometimes feeling unsafe, Jericho walls, guarded, insecurities, low self-esteem, dependence, self-sabotage, control, difficulties committing, afraid to be vulnerable - (Jealousy, trust, fear of being alone, guilt, trying too hard to please)
- **In Work**: Anxiety, overachiever, lack of commitment, unstable - (Felt like being in one place too long would make me feel trapped)
- **In Friendships:** Inability to be dependable or vulnerable, inconsistent availability, anti-social to avoid too much closeness - (Uncomfortable in larger groups or social events)
- **In my Health**: Overeating or undereating, sweet cravings, bingeing - (Emotional-eating and weight gain leading to insecurities around body and shame)

This list could go on and on but what I want you to understand is that unacknowledged pain lives very loud, even when it's quiet. It doesn't matter whether the trauma you experienced was sexual

Acknowledge How You Feel!

or something else, unhealed trauma will play out somewhere in your life because you will make decisions and create ideologies from that pain. When you don't acknowledge the things of your past, you create barriers and walls that make it almost impossible for others to break.

Unacknowledged pain creates fear, insecurities, depression, anxieties, trust issues, guards, inconsistencies and develops un-forgiveness in your own heart. It even creates sicknesses within your body! **James 5:16 says**, "Confess your sins to one another and pray for one another, that you may be healed."

The first step in getting to a place of healing is acknowledging where you are so that you may confess even if the trauma happened to you, and acknowledge how it made you feel. When you don't acknowledge your experiences, you take away the ability for you to process those feelings. Unprocessed hurt shows up as brokenness, emotional numbness or detachments, isolation, anxiety, low confidence, triggers, and creates extensive roots.

Many individuals have been trained to not say anything and ignore the pain, but sweeping your trauma under the rug is not God's desire. You can't hide and pretend that it never existed because the results will leave you in a space where you are carrying a burden that wasn't meant for you to carry. It will make it impossible for you to be your full authentic self. Silence is the plan of the enemy, not God's plan. Whether the pain came from daddy issues, church hurts, a death, family betrayal, relationship issues, infidelities, friendship, or life struggles, it is your responsibility to acknowledge, forgive, and release the pain.

Depending on how badly someone or something has hurt you, it can seem difficult to release, but ask yourself, "Why am I holding on to hurt in the first place?" Healing is your portion! Don't hold onto something that is not meant for you to carry, and remember that you don't have to heal alone!

Let me first acknowledge and say that I am so sorry for the thing you experienced that caused you pain. With that said, allow me to congratulate you on doing what is necessary to heal from the brokenness. Regardless of what you have or are experiencing, life might be "lifing," but God will still be God. **Luke 17:1-10** lets you know that stumbling blocks will happen and people will offend you but you have the power to forgive them seventy times more no matter how badly they have offended you. Give yourself permission to acknowledge the pain so that you can confess it, forgive it, and be healed from it. Remember God heals the brokenhearted and binds up your wounds even if your offender still offends. Forgiveness is not for them, it is to free your own heart of the attachment from the hurts it caused you.

Prayer:

Hey God, Thank you for showing me that you are far from anyone who has ever hurt me in my past. You have shown me time and time again that I can trust in you. Help me to acknowledge that I have been hurt many times by people whom I have trusted and loved but I can forgive them. Help me to walk through the process so that I may be proactive in my healing. Help me to understand my triggers. Give me the strength to not get lost in my emotions and to understand more about who I am. You have been my healer and you have the power to restore me, and for that, I am truly grateful! Thank you for all that you will do and continue to do. In Jesus name!

Activity

1. Create a list of everyone or anything you can think of that has ever caused you pain.
2. Acknowledge exactly what they did to hurt you.
3. Write out how those individuals affected you.
4. At the end write, "(Their name), I forgive you for <u>(whatever you did)</u>"
5. Write how how you were able to bounce back from what they did and an accomplishment you gained from it.
6. Release the situation to God in prayer and begin the process of healing.

Example: "John Doe, I forgive you for violating me when I was 8. What you did caused me to feel so much pain that for a while I was not able to trust people. What you did broke me but because of God I have been restored. I am now on my healing journey and able to share my story to help others. I release you from my heart and give it to God.

_____

_____

_____

_____

_____

_____

_____

_____

My Take-away's

1.
2.
3.
4.
5.

DEVOTIONAL NOTES

_____

_____

_____

_____

Top Three Affirmations

★ _____
★ _____
★ _____

Define your goals

▶ _____
▶ _____
▶ _____
▶ _____
▶ _____
▶ _____
▶ _____
▶ _____
▶ _____
▶ _____
▶ _____
▶ _____
▶ _____

Self Care Plans ✅ ❌

1. _____
2. _____
3. _____
4. _____
5. _____
6. _____

Prayer Focus ✅ ❌

1. _____
2. _____
3. _____
4. _____
5. _____
6. _____

Notes

BRAIN DUMP

DATE / /

Hey God, I'm busy a lot! Help me to be intentional.

CLEAR YOUR MIND!
What are all the things I can't stop thinking about?

HIGH PRIORITY
These are my non-negotiables, they have to get done!

LOW PRIORITY
These are important, but can wait.

FREE THOUGHTS
Remember to give yourself grace! You can't be everything to everyone. Fill up your cup and pour from the overflow.

5 Minutes of Meditation

S M T W TH F S

Breathe before writing

INHALE EXHALE INHALE EXHALE INHALE EXHALE

I'm intentionally meditating on?

* _____
* _____
* _____
* _____
* _____

Describe your feelings. You can draw or write.

Expose meditation lies!

Sometimes, we think about things that are not true. Write down a truth to a lie you heard while meditating and confirm it with a scripture.

Example: I expose the lie that I'm not good enough because God says that I am fearfully and wonderfully made.

This Week's Highlight

Things that you overcame:

_____
_____
_____
_____

My Action Step:

_____
_____

"This book of the law shall not depart out of thy mouth; but thou shalt meditate therein day and night." Joshua 1:8

Your mind should be clear. It's time to focus and just write.

Hey God, Can We Talk?   Date:

Your mind should be clear. It's time to focus and just write.

Hey God, Can We Talk?   Date:

Your mind should be clear. It's time to focus and just write.

Hey God, Can We Talk?   Date:

Your mind should be clear. It's time to focus and just write.

Hey God, Can We Talk?   Date:

Your mind should be clear. It's time to focus and just write.

Hey God, Can We Talk?   Date:

THE SCRIPTURE THAT KEPT ME ▶

WHAT CAN I DO DIFFERENTLY NEXT TIME?

▶

▶

▶

HOW CAN I REWARD MYSELF?

▶

▶

▶

WHAT WERE MY CHALLENGES? WAS I HARD ON MYSELF? DID I GIVE MYSELF GRACE? HAVE I FORGIVEN MYSELF? LET'S TALK TO GOD ABOUT IT!

Am I Triggered?

Trauma triggers are unpredictable pain reminders! Individuals can be triggered by a person, a place, a thing, or a situation. It could be a result of what someone said, a memory, a specific smell, sight, taste, or even sound. Triggers are unexpected emotional responses to a certain situation that are usually negative from a previous traumatic experience.

What are some signs of being triggered?

- Feeling intense emotions such as anger, sadness, anxiety, or fear.
- Physical signs like your heart beating fast, getting sweaty, trembling, finding it hard to breathe.
- Not being in control of your feelings, like when you can't stop being mad or sad.
- Struggling to express yourself clearly or communicate effectively, due to overwhelmed emotions.
- Defensive Behavior, feeling attacked or criticized, even if that wasn't the intention of the conversation or situation.
- Withdrawal or shut down, becoming unresponsive or emotionally distant, or avoidance behavior.
- Irritability, agitated, or snappy with others or uncontrollable crying.
- Negative Self-Talk, self-criticism, or expressing negative thoughts about yourself, your abilities, or your self-worth.
- Repetitive or Obsessive Thoughts which can lead to rumination and distress.
- Disconnection from Reality experiencing dissociation.
- *Worst Case: Self-harm, or self-destructive behaviors like self-harm or substance abuse as a way to cope

What are some examples of triggers?

- Hearing a favorite song after a bad break-up. Could be a song you both enjoyed that reminded you of the experience.
- Withdrawing from family during a holiday season because it reminds you of a lost loved one.
- Seeing an ex in a new relationship could trigger an intense emotional response of mixed emotions.
- Seeing a random father playing in a park with his children could trigger the absence of your father not being present.
- Not responding to messages promptly could trigger feelings of insecurity and anxiety.
- Mentioning an ex to your current partner can be triggering.
- Forgetting a birthday or anniversary could lead to being triggered.
- Financial disagreements have always been a major trigger for conflicts in their marriage
- Staying out late with friends and not communicating or not spending quality time with partner can be triggering.

What can I do if I'm being triggered?

1. Pay attention to how you feel. If you are feeling a sudden change in emotions that is beyond your control, acknowledge it.
2. Create a preventative measure to cope with the reaction and plan ahead. For example, if you know you are going to a party and your ex will be there, prepare a coping mechanism in the event that you see them.
3. Have your moment, use that moment to relax your mind. Use the breathing chart on the 5-minute meditation page to practice the inhale and exhale technique to catch yourself. Notice how you feel in that moment and remember it.
4. Develop a routine to practice self-care and take care of yourself.
5. Pray and give the burden of your triggers to God to carry.
6. Journal your thoughts. It is important to keep track of what it is you are going through so that you can recognize patterns and behaviors. This will help you to be more controlled and prepared if there is a next time.

TRIGGER ASSESSMENT

Please rate the following statements on a scale of 1 to 5, where 1 represents "strongly disagree" and 5 represents "strongly agree."

1 2 3 4 5	Are you experiencing intense emotions right now, such as anger, fear, sadness, or anxiety?
1 2 3 4 5	Is your heart rate elevated, or are you experiencing physical symptoms like tension, sweating, or trembling?
1 2 3 4 5	Are you having negative or irrational thoughts that are difficult to control?
1 2 3 4 5	Are you feeling a strong urge to react impulsively or defensively?
1 2 3 4 5	Are you ruminating on past events or experiences that relate to the current situation?
1 2 3 4 5	Is your ability to focus or concentrate impaired because of your emotional state?
1 2 3 4 5	Are you experiencing an overwhelming desire to avoid or escape the situation?
1 2 3 4 5	Do you find it challenging to communicate calmly and effectively with others in the present moment?
1 2 3 4 5	Are you experiencing a sense of being threatened or unsafe, even if the situation is not objectively dangerous?
1 2 3 4 5	Are you aware that your emotional response is disproportionate to the current situation or seems to be linked to past experiences or triggers?

Calculate your average rating: Add up your ratings for all the statements.

Scoring:

Total Score 1-9: Very low likelihood of being triggered. Your emotional response to the situation is generally well-managed, and you are likely in control of your emotions.

Total Score 10-19: Low likelihood of being triggered. Your emotional response suggests that you may be somewhat affected by the situation, but you are generally in control of your emotions.

Total Score 20-29: Moderate likelihood of being triggered. Your emotional response indicates that you are moderately affected by the situation, and it's worth paying attention to your emotions and potentially implementing some coping strategies.

Total Score 30-39: Moderate to high likelihood of being triggered. Your emotional response suggests that you are significantly affected by the situation, and it's important to recognize this and consider taking steps to manage your emotions effectively.

Total Score 40-50: High likelihood of being triggered. Your emotional response indicates that you are very likely being triggered by the current situation or event. It's essential to recognize this and take immediate steps to manage your emotions effectively, such as using coping techniques, seeking support, or removing yourself from the triggering situation if possible.

Conclusion:

I'm so excited that you are putting in the work to understand your triggers. When you truly understand what causes you to be triggered then you can be proactive in getting the healing that you need. Acknowledging allows you to become self aware as you go through the continued process. If you are triggered, complete a meditational breathing in the section of this book.

⭐ Disclaimer:

This assessment is intended for informational and self-reflective purposes only. It is not a substitute for professional counseling, therapy, or advice. Use it as a starting point for self-reflection and personal growth, and be open to adapting your approach as you continue to explore what triggers you. Results should be viewed as a guide and not as a definitive diagnosis or solution. Please consult a qualified professional for personalized support if needed.

Step workbook Three

Hey God, Help me to see me as your image.

Explore what it means to be created in God's image. Rediscover your divine identity and the purpose He has placed in you.

LET'S CHECK IN

DATE _____

TOP 3 THINGS I WAS INTENTIONAL ABOUT
- _____
- _____
- _____

THIS WEEK I FELT?

WHAT WERE MY PATTERNS?

WHAT DO I NEED TO FOCUS ON NEXT?
_____
_____
_____
_____

WAS I TRIGGERED?

IN WHAT WAY WILL I SHOW UP FOR ME?

MY RANKING OF THE WEEK
★ ★ ★ ★ ★

LET'S CREATE A PLAN

MONDAY   TUESDAY   WEDNESDAY

THURSDAY   FRIDAY   SATURDAY

APPOINTMENT TIMES   SUNDAY   TASK/REMINDERS

KEEP GOING!

Misc. doodle

TO-DO'S

PHOTO/reminders?

Just living my best life.

~ STEP 3 ~
HEY GOD, HELP ME TO SEE ME AS YOUR IMAGE.

Affirm - "I am created as the image of God!"

Gen: 1:27 NIV
"So God created mankind in his own image, in the image of God he created them;"

You may hear quite often that you are made in God's image, but have you ever really sat down to understand what that truly means? The reality is that understanding this could take years, maybe even a lifetime, and you'd probably only touch the tip of the iceberg with your own understanding. What can be understood is that knowing even a little will help you to learn more about who you are. Why is this important? Because your identity is wrapped up in God's image and who He created you to be.

The first understanding of being created in God's image is learning that all you had to do was exist to qualify as an image bearer. You didn't have to think about it or do anything special. You didn't have to be the most educated in the room, your skin color didn't matter, your sexual orientation didn't matter, your religion didn't matter, your size, whether you were big or small didn't matter because none of that determined your worthiness of being an image bearer. All you had to do was be born and baam... you are the image! I need you to sit on that for a moment! Selah!

In the beginning, God created. He created light in the darkness, the sky, dry land and plants, the sun, moon and stars, the seas, birds in the sky, animals and then He created you. God was intentional with everything He created. He spoke everything into existence, but when it came to man He formed you. He used His hands to create the framework of a man, out of the dust of the ground, and then He used His breath to breathe in you the breath of life.

I want to put this in perspective. I have three children but I want to talk about how it was when I gave birth to my firstborn. I felt like at that time it was one of my greatest accomplishments.

You are the Reflection!

She was the splitting image of me. People would constantly remind me of how much she looked like me. Because she was my child, I showed her love, I nurtured her, and I took the best care of her. I tried my best to protect her from anything harmful. I got angry if someone attempted to mistreat her in any way. I comforted her when she was sad, and supported her when she achieved her goals. I was her biggest cheerleader. As a parent I did what I could to make her happy. As she grew older and began to experience life, I taught her lessons to the best of my ability. She was kind because I taught her kindness, she showed others love because I taught her to love others.

I had an expectation that she would implement the principles I taught her out in the world. If she didn't make a good decision or did something I didn't approve of, I would look at where I went wrong. As a parent I thought of what I could have done differently to help her make better decisions. Her behavior was a reflection of me, and now with my boys I do the same thing. I want for them to go out in the world and apply the principles that I taught them at home to represent me. When she went off to college, people would tell me how good of a parent I was. When she messed up, people would tell me what they thought I should have done. Her decisions whether good or bad, with or without her knowledge were a direct reflection of me. She applied principles from her upbringing to make decisions either intentionally or unintentionally. This is the very example of being an image bearer.

Think about the relationship you have with your parent(s) and how you unintentionally made many of your decisions based on how they taught you. Regardless of how you turned out, you most likely made decisions that reflected how you were brought up. God created you in His image and used His breath to give you life as a reflection to Him. It was the intention of God to fill the earth with image bearers. His desire was for you to grow up reflecting Him.

Unfortunately, there was an enemy called satan, who made it his absolute goal to change what God's image would look like. The goal was to get you to act outside of your character so that you could change the way that God is perceived. If the enemy can get you to act out because you were abused, violated, lost a loved one, was cheated on and so forth, then mission accomplished. The absolute goal of satan is to use the things that happen to you in order to delay your purpose and make you feel as though you are far from God. He wants to make you believe that you don't look like God at all. The enemy wants to take your experiences and use them against you in a way that pushes you towards violating God. He wants to change your behavior so that it doesn't reflect how God created you to be.

I Am God's Image!

The reality is that as long as people are able to decide, sin will coexist. As you go through life, you are going to be faced with the ability to make decisions. The job is to try and make you forget all that God has taught you. If you are a true follower of God, your decisions should be based on the relationship that you have with God. This means that you should be using principles that are rooted in God as a foundation to respond to others. As a guideline, you will know if you are applying those principles because they would exhibit the fruit as discussed in Galatians 5:22-23. "But the fruit of the Spirit is love, joy, peace, forbearance, kindness, goodness, faithfulness, gentleness and self-control. Against such things there is no law."

In other words, how can your decisions reflect love, joy, peace, patience, kindness, goodness, faithfulness, gentleness and self-control? God exhibited all of these attributes when He created you, and it is His desire that you demonstrate these fruits in your everyday lives because it represents His image. Are you an image bearer? The question I would propose is how can understanding God's image help you to learn more about you, so that you can make better decisions even when things in life just keep happening?

Prayer:

Hey God, I first want to thank you for helping me understand that I was created in Your image. If I can be honest, there are many times when I struggle with this concept. How can I reflect you when so many things in my life happen? I sometimes don't feel as close to you as I should. I have often times allowed the experiences I've had to pull me away from you because I didn't understand why they were happening. I thank you that even though I felt what I felt, you never left or forsaken me. You came to search for me every time just to show me that I am a product of you. You see me for who I am and not my life struggles. I want to be a better version of myself. I want to be more like you. I want to reflect you. Help me to be more loving, patient and kind. Help me to be gentle and practice self-control. Help me to be faithful to you and others. I want to experience joy and peace in all areas of my life. I might not be fully where I need to be but I am ready to begin this journey from where I am. I am ready to push past my feelings and emotions to just start. Thank you for leading me.

In Jesus name!

Activity

1. Materials: A notepad or phone for tracking your progress.
2. Instructions: Choose one fruit of the Spirit each week (e.g., start with Love). Set a personal challenge related to that quality.
3. Write down your experiences and any difficulties you encounter.
4. Reflection: At the end of the week, review how you did. What was easy? What was challenging? How did focusing on that fruit impact your mindset?

Example: For "Patience," you might challenge yourself to wait calmly in line without checking your phone. For "Kindness," you could make it a goal to perform a random act of kindness each day.

_____
_____
_____
_____
_____

My Take-away's

1.
2.
3.
4.
5.

DEVOTIONAL NOTES

_____
_____
_____
_____

Top Three Affirmations

★ _____
★ _____
★ _____

Define your goals

▶ _____
▶ _____
▶ _____
▶ _____
▶ _____
▶ _____
▶ _____
▶ _____
▶ _____
▶ _____
▶ _____
▶ _____

Self Care Plans ✅ ❌

1. _____
2. _____
3. _____
4. _____
5. _____
6. _____

Prayer Focus ✅ ❌

1. _____
2. _____
3. _____
4. _____
5. _____
6. _____

Notes

BRAIN DUMP

DATE / /

Hey God, I'm busy a lot! Help me to be intentional.

CLEAR YOUR MIND!
What are all the things I can't stop thinking about?

-
-
-
-
-

HIGH PRIORITY
These are my non-negotiables, they have to get done!

-
-
-

LOW PRIORITY
These are important, but can wait.

-
-
-

FREE THOUGHTS
Remember to give yourself grace! You can't be everything to everyone. Fill up your cup and pour from the overflow.

5 Minutes of Meditation

S M T W TH F S

Breathe before writing

INHALE EXHALE INHALE EXHALE INHALE EXHALE

I'm intentionally meditating on?
* _____
* _____
* _____
* _____
* _____

Describe your feelings. You can draw or write.

My Action Step:
_____
_____

Expose meditation lies!

Sometimes, we think about things that are not true. Write down a truth to a lie you heard while meditating and confirm it with a scripture.

Example: I expose the lie that I'm not good enough because God says that I am fearfully and wonderfully made.

This Week's Highlight

Things that you overcame:
_____
_____
_____
_____

"This book of the law shall not depart out of thy mouth; but thou shalt meditate therein day and night." Joshua 1:8

Your mind should be clear. It's time to focus and just write.

Hey God, Can We Talk?   Date:

Your mind should be clear. It's time to focus and just write.

Hey God, Can We Talk? Date:

Your mind should be clear. It's time to focus and just write.

Hey God, Can We Talk?   Date:

Your mind should be clear. It's time to focus and just write.

Hey God, Can We Talk?   Date:

Your mind should be clear. It's time to focus and just write.

Hey God, Can We Talk?   Date:

THE SCRIPTURE THAT KEPT ME ▶

WHAT CAN I DO DIFFERENTLY NEXT TIME?

▶

▶

▶

HOW CAN I REWARD MYSELF?

▶

▶

▶

WHAT WERE MY CHALLENGES? WAS I HARD ON MYSELF? DID I GIVE MYSELF GRACE? HAVE I FORGIVEN MYSELF? LET'S TALK TO GOD ABOUT IT!

CAN YOU HELP THIS ADAM AND EVE FIND THEIR WAY BACK TO THE GARDEN?

"SO GOD CREATED MANKIND IN HIS OWN IMAGE, IN THE IMAGE OF GOD HE CREATED THEM; MALE AND FEMALE HE CREATED THEM." GEN.1:27

YOU WERE CREATED IN THE IMAGE OF GOD.

WORD SEARCH

Can you find all the words related to God's Image?

h	o	l	y	s	p	i	r	i	t	r	e	y	l	e
w	x	o	g	o	d	h	e	a	d	t	n	q	x	u
f	b	y	s	i	a	c	e	j	b	y	m	p	n	t
w	o	n	k	o	t	r	m	i	y	t	l	o	g	i
m	k	s	i	h	j	h	b	p	p	o	n	e	s	s
b	s	i	o	u	a	r	o	n	r	e	e	n	y	n
e	l	m	n	k	b	m	d	e	g	r	f	g	a	o
a	b	i	e	n	j	o	y	g	h	t	o	n	d	i
r	i	r	n	d	s	t	a	l	i	r	y	s	a	t
e	f	r	e	e	d	o	m	t	b	i	r	g	f	c
r	e	o	s	i	o	d	i	t	y	n	p	b	i	e
i	n	r	s	a	f	f	e	c	t	i	o	n	a	l
c	i	m	a	g	e	i	d	e	n	t	i	t	y	f
e	l	p	q	w	n	o	i	t	p	y	r	t	t	e
t	f	u	p	i	h	s	n	o	i	t	a	l	e	r

Enjoy	Relationship	Affection	Oneness	Image	Reflection
Embody	To Know	Freedom	Trinity	Bearer	Holy Spirit
Explore	Deep	YADA	Godhead	Mirror	Identity

68

My Image

What would you have said to yourself knowing the struggles you were going to face? Find a pre-trauma photo of yourself and coach them through the things you know they will go through. How would you encourage that version of you? What was the advice you needed to hear? Let your younger self know that you see them, that you hear them and that they are valued. Convince them that they were made in the image of God.

Paste an old photo of yourself here.

Step
workbook
Four

Hey God, Fix me where I am broken.

Focus on restoration. Surrender your brokenness to God and allow Him to bring renewal and wholeness into your life.

LET'S CHECK IN

DATE _____

TOP 3 THINGS I WAS INTENTIONAL ABOUT
- _____
- _____
- _____

THIS WEEK I FELT?

WHAT WERE MY PATTERNS?

WHAT DO I NEED TO FOCUS ON NEXT?
_____
_____
_____
_____

WAS I TRIGGERED?

IN WHAT WAY WILL I SHOW UP FOR ME?

MY RANKING OF THE WEEK
☆ ☆ ☆ ☆ ☆

LET'S CREATE A PLAN

MONDAY

TUESDAY

WEDNESDAY

THURSDAY

FRIDAY

SATURDAY

APPOINTMENT TIMES

-
-
-
-
-
-

SUNDAY

TASK/REMINDERS

KEEP GOING!

Misc. doodle

TO-DO'S

PHOTO/reminders?

Just living my best life.

73

~ STEP 4 ~

HEY GOD, FIX ME WHERE I AM BROKEN.

Affirm - "God will meet me where I'm at."

John 8:1-11 NIV

"but Jesus went to the Mount of Olives. At dawn he appeared again in the temple courts, where all the people gathered around him, and he sat down to teach them. The teachers of the law and the Pharisees brought in a woman caught in adultery. They made her stand before the group and said to Jesus, "Teacher, this woman was caught in the act of adultery. In the Law Moses commanded us to stone such women. Now what do you say?" They were using this question as a trap, in order to have a basis for accusing him. But Jesus bent down and started to write on the ground with his finger. When they kept on questioning him, he straightened up and said to them, "Let any one of you who is without sin be the first to throw a stone at her." Again he stooped down and wrote on the ground. At this, those who heard began to go away one at a time, the older ones first, until only Jesus was left, with the woman still standing there. Jesus straightened up and asked her, "Woman, where are they? Has no one condemned you? "No one, sir," she said. "Then neither do I condemn you," Jesus declared. "Go now and leave your life of sin."

Have you ever been in a place where you have been so broken, you weren't even sure if the pieces could be put back together? I have... many times! In fact, what many don't know about me is that I would have been what the Bible called a whoremonger, a liar, cheater, and a thief. I have done all the things and some of those things I didn't think I could bounce back from. I've been told I "act" like dudes in relationships and that I would have to leave town and start all over to be taken seriously because I was in those 'streets'. I've been told by friends that it sucked to be my friend. I've been told that I was cold, heartless, and that I "acted" like I didn't care. The list could go on. The reality was that I was broken and living my brokenness out loud, just like the adulterous woman.

It was quite obvious that this adulterous woman was living in sin for some time. She was comfortable in her sin. I'm sure that the Pharisees didn't have to work hard to catch her in the act. They watched her live in sin and used her sin as a benefit to them. I could even assume that to catch her in the act could have meant that she was even set up. They watched, they plotted and they waited for her to be in a vulnerable state to defile and catch her. She was naked and ashamed and they took her into the public to make a display of her error.

There is no condemnation for those who are in Christ Jesus.

We don't know her story, her background, or the reason she felt that what she did was an option. I could only imagine what it may have felt like to have her life be put on display. I remember many times doing the walk of shame after an encounter with someone who I should not have been with, and me being in private, I still felt some type of way. Thinking about the public damage and humiliation it likely caused would be an understatement. For the adulterous woman, it had to be difficult because it would have brought to reality the very thing she tried to hide.

With no good intentions, the Pharisee's took her to Jesus! Selah... They said, "We caught this woman in the act!" I'm sure she stood there betrayed, embarrassed, and ashamed. They took her out of that place as if she was nothing but a prop to be used in order to entrap Jesus. With the adulterous woman knowing the consequences, she was probably afraid and feeling helpless all at the same time. She knew that sleeping with that man could be death if they got caught, and yet still she risked it all. I sometimes wondered the circumstances of why she did what she did, but more importantly, I wondered why they chose her. I believe that they felt her sin was so great that Jesus would have no choice but to respond to it. They knew they needed her, but Jesus had a certain place in His heart for broken women. The Pharisees knew He would respond to her sin but they didn't anticipate that He would respond the way He did. Jesus had a different plan. He knelt down with a posture of grace and understanding. He didn't make her feel condemned because of her irresponsible decisions. Instead, He gave those who accused her of breaking the law permission to stone her if they had never sinned in their life, and not one person could. Why? Because we all fall short!

What I love about this story so much was the posture of Jesus in the midst of her sin. He got down to her level to show her that there was nothing that she couldn't be healed from. He showed her compassion and forgiveness in just one kneel. He sacrificed Himself to show her that in spite of her sin, she was still valuable. He didn't disregard what she did, instead God exposed her sin, showed her love, and told her to go and sin no more.

There are some of you who are reading this who have been broken in more ways than you can count. That brokenness may have left you trying to fill many different voids, feeling so many different ways, and making decisions you wouldn't typically make. You may not even recognize 'you' anymore. You may even find yourself acting outside of your character, or trying to discover if what you are doing is who you truly are. I want to remind you of the grace of God. It doesn't matter what you have done in your past or your present, His mercy still exist. His grace will bend down to reach you in whatever sin you are in because He see's you. He see's your hurts, your pains, and He knows your why. Remember you are His image. There is no condemnation for those who are in Christ. Wholeness is your portion.

Hey God,

As I sit here and think about the sins I've done, the things that made me look less than your image, I sit in gratitude because you didn't punish me in the way I deserved. You've showed me that I am more valuable than I feel about myself. You meet me where I am even though I am at rock bottom. For this, I am grateful. I repent for all the things that I've done or continuously do. I want to thank you for restoring me and showing me that I don't have to live my life in broken pieces. Thank you for showing me that you can make me whole again. Thank you for not condemning me. I surrender Lord. From this day forward, with your help, I will humbly make a conscious effort to go out, and sin no more!

In Jesus name!

Activity

1. Materials: Pen
2. Instructions: Is there a time you have ever felt like the adulterous woman? Write a list of things that you can relate to and place the list into the jar or box, symbolizing giving your burdens to God.
3. Pray the below scripture once you have filled your jar. Romans 10:8-13 NIV

"But what does it say? "The word is near you; it is in your mouth and in your heart," that is, the message concerning faith that we proclaim: If you declare with your mouth, "Jesus is Lord," and believe in your heart that God raised him from the dead, you will be saved. For it is with your heart that you believe and are justified, and it is with your mouth that you profess your faith and are saved. As Scripture says, "Anyone who believes in him will never be put to shame." For there is no difference between Jew and Gentile—the same Lord is Lord of all and richly blesses all who call on him, for, "Everyone who calls on the name of the Lord will be saved."

THE *Release it* JAR

Things I want to release to God.

- Food will no longer be an idol.
- I release to God all of my addictions.

My Take-away's

1.
2.
3.
4.
5.

DEVOTIONAL NOTES

Top Three Affirmations

★ _____

★ _____

★ _____

Define your goals

▶ _____

▶ _____

▶ _____

▶ _____

▶ _____

▶ _____

▶ _____

▶ _____

▶ _____

▶ _____

▶ _____

▶ _____

Self Care Plans ✅ ❌

1.
2.
3.
4.
5.
6.

Prayer Focus ✅ ❌

1.
2.
3.
4.
5.
6.

Notes

BRAIN DUMP

DATE / /

Hey God, I'm busy a lot! Help me to be intentional.

CLEAR YOUR MIND!
What are all the things I can't stop thinking about?

-
-
-
-
-
-

HIGH PRIORITY
These are my non-negotiables, they have to get done!

-
-
-

LOW PRIORITY
These are important, but can wait.

-
-
-

FREE THOUGHTS
Remember to give yourself grace! You can't be everything to everyone. Fill up your cup and pour from the overflow.

80

5 Minutes of Meditation

S M T W TH F S

Breathe before writing

INHALE | EXHALE | INHALE | EXHALE | INHALE | EXHALE

I'm intentionally meditating on?

* _____
* _____
* _____
* _____
* _____

Describe your feelings. You can draw or write.

Expose meditation lies!

Sometimes, we think about things that are not true. Write down a truth to a lie you heard while meditating and confirm it with a scripture.

Example: I expose the lie that I'm not good enough because God says that I am fearfully and wonderfully made.

This Week's Highlight

Things that you overcame:

_____
_____
_____

My Action Step:

_____
_____

"This book of the law shall not depart out of thy mouth; but thou shalt meditate therein day and night." Joshua 1:8

Your mind should be clear. It's time to focus and just write.

Hey God, Can We Talk?   Date:

Your mind should be clear. It's time to focus and just write.

Hey God, Can We Talk?   Date:

Your mind should be clear. It's time to focus and just write.

Hey God, Can We Talk? Date:

Your mind should be clear. It's time to focus and just write.

Hey God, Can We Talk?   Date:

Your mind should be clear. It's time to focus and just write.

Hey God, Can We Talk?   Date:

THE SCRIPTURE THAT KEPT ME ▶

WHAT CAN I DO DIFFERENTLY NEXT TIME?

▶

▶

▶

HOW CAN I REWARD MYSELF?

▶

▶

▶

WHAT WERE MY CHALLENGES? WAS I HARD ON MYSELF? DID I GIVE MYSELF GRACE? HAVE I FORGIVEN MYSELF? LET'S TALK TO GOD ABOUT IT!

Let's put the broken puzzle pieces back together!

INSTRUCTIONS: Use the below word box to fill in puzzle pieces by answering the questions given. There are no wrong answers.

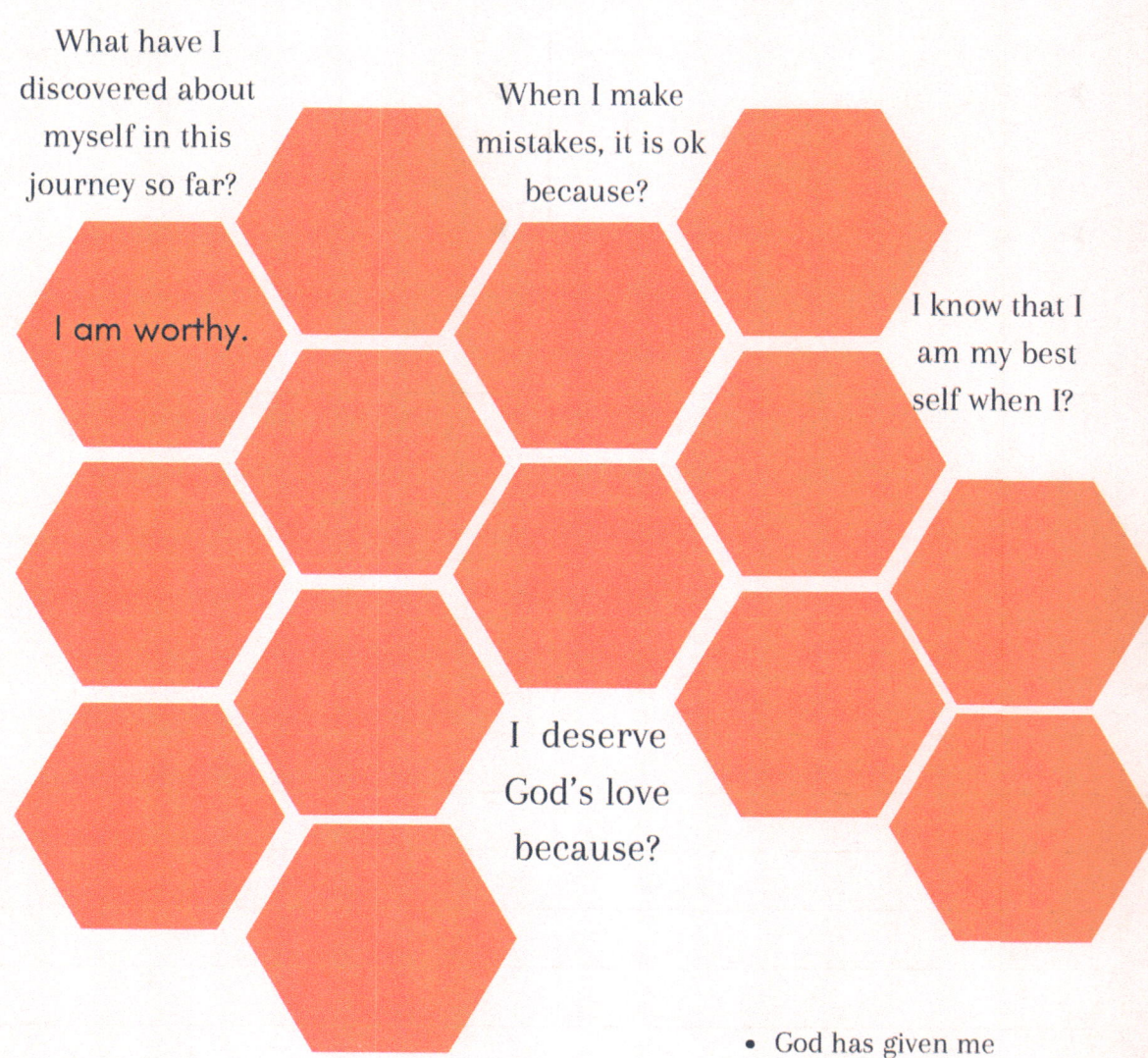

What have I discovered about myself in this journey so far?

When I make mistakes, it is ok because?

I am worthy.

I know that I am my best self when I?

I deserve God's love because?

- ~~I am worthy~~
- I am capable of growth
- I have a purpose
- I'm stronger than I feel
- Healing is a process
- God don't play about me
- I walk in alignment
- I will prioritize self-care
- I help others to grow
- God loves me
- God has given me unconditional grace
- I am created in God's image
- I will maintain healthy boundaries
- I fully love and accept myself

88

Step workbook Five

Hey God, is pleasure my birthright?

Learn to embrace joy and God-given desires without guilt or shame. Reflect on the goodness of God's gifts and His plan for your fulfillment.

This Month, I Declare That:

DECLARATIONS

1. I am fearfully and wonderfully made, and I will walk in confidence (Psalm 139:14).
2. God's plans for me are good, and I will embrace the hope and future He has for me (Jeremiah 29:11).
3. I can do all things through Christ who strengthens me, and nothing will hold me back (Philippians 4:13).
4. I am a new creation in Christ, and I will step boldly into the new things He is doing (2 Corinthians 5:17).
5. The Lord is my shepherd, and I will lack nothing this month (Psalm 23:1).
6. I will walk by faith and not by sight, trusting God's perfect plan (2 Corinthians 5:7).
7. No weapon formed against me shall prosper; I will live in victory (Isaiah 54:17).
8. I am more than a conqueror, and I will overcome every challenge with God's love (Romans 8:37).
9. The peace of God will guard my heart and mind, and I will dwell in perfect peace (Philippians 4:7).
10. I am rooted and grounded in love, and I will know the fullness of God's presence (Ephesians 3:17-19).
11. I have the mind of Christ, and my thoughts are aligned with His truth (1 Corinthians 2:16).
12. God is working all things together for my good, and I will trust Him completely (Romans 8:28).
13. I am the righteousness of God in Christ, and I will live a life that reflects His glory (2 Corinthians 5:21).
14. Greater is He that is in me than he that is in the world, and I will walk in boldness (1 John 4:4).
15. The joy of the Lord is my strength, and I will rejoice in every season (Nehemiah 8:10).

| Goals |

This month, I walk in faith, love, victory, and purpose, fully trusting in God's promises! ✨🙏

LET'S CHECK IN

DATE _____

TOP 3 THINGS I WAS INTENTIONAL ABOUT

- _____
- _____
- _____

WHAT WERE MY PATTERNS?

THIS WEEK I FELT?

WHAT DO I NEED TO FOCUS ON NEXT?

_____
_____
_____
_____

WAS I TRIGGERED?

IN WHAT WAY WILL I SHOW UP FOR ME?

MY RANKING OF THE WEEK

★ ★ ★ ★ ★

LET'S CREATE A PLAN

MONDAY | TUESDAY | WEDNESDAY

THURSDAY | FRIDAY | SATURDAY

APPOINTMENT TIMES | SUNDAY | TASK/REMINDERS

-
-
-
-
-
-

KEEP GOING!

Misc. doodle

TO-DO'S

PHOTO/reminders?

Just living my best life.

~ STEP 5 ~

HEY GOD, IS PLEASURE MY BIRTHRIGHT?

Affirm - "I'm worthy of pleasure!"

Isaiah 55:2 (NIV)
"Why spend money on what is not bread, and your labor on what does not satisfy? Listen, listen to me, and eat what is good, and you will delight in the richest of fare."

Did you know that there are people who don't believe that they deserve happiness? I get it, some people have experienced so many hardships that they have come to the conclusion that pleasure is somewhat impossible to achieve. Life will do that to you. It will make you feel that pleasure doesn't exist but I am here to tell you that it is your birthright. I know it may be difficult to see when "life be lifing," but when God created you, it was rooted in pleasure.

God designed you to experience joy, delight, and fulfillment as part of His perfect plan. The goal of the enemy has always been to make life so hard that it keeps you from experiencing it. The enemy wants to steal, kill and destroy you to the point where you don't acknowledge that pleasure exist, but it does. Although he may have had some small level of delusion, he won't after today! Pleasure aligns with God's nature. It reflects His goodness and holiness. He delighted in His creation when He created you. He wanted you to have so many moments where you could say, "This is good!"

Here is a thought, "I have come that you may have life and have it to the full." John 10:10. The life God desires for you is not just about survival but about thriving mentally, emotionally, spiritually, and physically. It's about abundance. Whenever I was going through something, my friends would say to me, "Tammy, you are a survivor!" I can honestly say I was tired of just surviving. After you have experienced so much, there are times when you ask, "when does it end?" I was tired of living my life in survival mode. At some point I wanted to just live. God wants us all to live an abundant life. This includes joy, peace, and fulfillment. Many times I would experience things and equivalate that with God and His abundance, but I had to learn that it is not the same.

You have to make a decision that God is enough.

Trials doesn't mean that you aren't living in abundance. True pleasure comes when you live in alignment with God's design for wholeness in mind, body, and spirit, regardless of what you experience. God wants you to be free from shame and brokenness because pleasure has been given to you whether you acknowledge that you have it or not.

To live means that you are already experiencing God's pleasure. To breathe means that you are able to experience the very pleasure of the breath of the Lord. The Bible says, "consider it pure joy, my brothers and sisters, whenever you face trials of many kinds, because you know that the testing of your faith produces perseverance. Let perseverance finish its work so that you may be mature and complete, not lacking anything." James 12-4 (NIV)

The fact that scripture is telling you to, "count it all joy," in your trials, means that it doesn't matter what your circumstance is, you have the ability to access pleasure. What else does that tell you? That pleasure is not a reflection of what you experience or how you feel because it was something that was given to you. You get to decide as an individual that you will accept the things of God to be pleasurable. You have to make a decision that God, and all that He has laid out for you can be enough for you; so that as you go through life, it doesn't make you feel less than what God has intended. It means that you have the ability to change your posture to an, "I get to do this," mindset. When God created Adam and Eve, He gave them access to abundance. They got to decide with the exception of one tree, what they wanted to eat, where they wanted to go. They got to enjoy touching, feeling, tasting, smelling, and hearing the voice of God. While in the garden they got to enjoy all of the five senses of a pleasurable experience.

You might be asking, "why am I not experiencing pleasure?" When you are living your life in sin, it separates you from experiencing the fullness of joy and replaces it with a counterfeit. Counterfeits only give you a temporary feeling of pleasure. In order to have lasting pleasure, it has to be rooted in the things of God. Repentance restores your ability to experience God-given pleasure.

Psalm 51:12 says, "Restore to me the joy of your salvation." God's forgiveness allows you to reclaim the joy and delight that are your birthright in Him. Don't allow the worlds perception of pleasure to distract you. The worlds perception will have you feeling empty. That's why things like depression, anxiety and mental illnesses are so high. The world will make you feel suicidal because you can't keep up. The world's idea of pleasure is not real. True pleasure can only be found when it is rooted in relationship with God. You deserve the opportunity to experience that type of pleasure.

Hey God,

I'm so grateful that your ways are not like my ways and your thoughts are not like my thoughts. I can admit that I had no idea what pleasure truly was. I allowed the world to define for me what was going to be pleasurable but true pleasure is rooted in you. It is something that you have given to me freely, in fact, it is my birthright. Help me to now understand what that means in you. Help me to understand how to experience the type of pleasure that fulfills. Help me to experience the type of pleasure that restores. I want to experience happiness in abundance regardless of my circumstance. I want to find joy in knowing the plans you have for me. Thank you for restoring me and giving me a fresh outlook of the life that was destined for me. It is only in you that I can find my joy and for that I am forever thankful.

In Jesus name!

Activity

God gave you the ability to enjoy things in life as long as it does not violate His word. Are you aware of what brings you pleasure? Create a list and write them down.

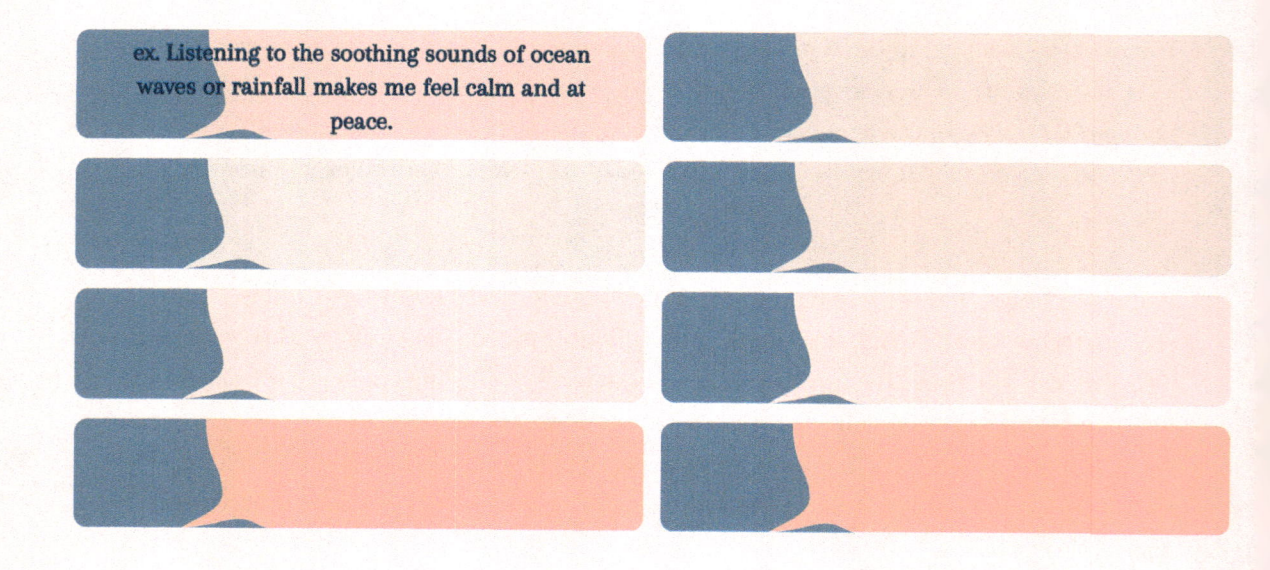

ex. Listening to the soothing sounds of ocean waves or rainfall makes me feel calm and at peace.

My Take-away's

1.
2.
3.
4.
5.

DEVOTIONAL NOTES

Top Three Affirmations

⭐ _____
⭐ _____
⭐ _____

Define your goals

▶ _____
▶ _____
▶ _____
▶ _____
▶ _____
▶ _____
▶ _____
▶ _____
▶ _____
▶ _____
▶ _____
▶ _____

Self Care Plans ✅ ❌

1. _____
2. _____
3. _____
4. _____
5. _____
6. _____

Prayer Focus ✅ ❌

1. _____
2. _____
3. _____
4. _____
5. _____
6. _____

Notes

98

BRAIN DUMP

DATE / /

Hey God, I'm busy a lot! Help me to be intentional.

CLEAR YOUR MIND!
What are all the things I can't stop thinking about?

-
-
-
-
-

HIGH PRIORITY
These are my non-negotiables, they have to get done!

-
-

LOW PRIORITY
These are important, but can wait.

-
-

FREE THOUGHTS
Remember to give yourself grace! You can't be everything to everyone. Fill up your cup and pour from the overflow.

5 Minutes of Meditation

S M T W TH F S

Breathe before writing

INHALE EXHALE INHALE EXHALE INHALE EXHALE

I'm intentionally meditating on?
* _____
* _____
* _____
* _____
* _____

Describe your feelings. You can draw or write.

Expose meditation lies!

Sometimes, we think about things that are not true. Write down a truth to a lie you heard while meditating and confirm it with a scripture.

Example: I expose the lie that I'm not good enough because God says that I am fearfully and wonderfully made.

This Week's Highlight

Things that you overcame:
_____
_____
_____
_____
_____

My Action Step:
_____
_____

"This book of the law shall not depart out of thy mouth; but thou shalt meditate therein day and night." Joshua 1:8

Your mind should be clear. It's time to focus and just write.

Hey God, Can We Talk? Date:

Your mind should be clear. It's time to focus and just write.

Hey God, Can We Talk? Date:

Your mind should be clear. It's time to focus and just write.

Hey God, Can We Talk?   Date:

Your mind should be clear. It's time to focus and just write.

Hey God, Can We Talk? Date:

Your mind should be clear. It's time to focus and just write.

Hey God, Can We Talk?   Date:

THE SCRIPTURE THAT KEPT ME ▶

WHAT CAN I DO DIFFERENTLY NEXT TIME?
▶
▶
▶

HOW CAN I REWARD MYSELF?
▶
▶
▶

WHAT WERE MY CHALLENGES? WAS I HARD ON MYSELF? DID I GIVE MYSELF GRACE? HAVE I FORGIVEN MYSELF? LET'S TALK TO GOD ABOUT IT!

PLEASURE ASSESSMENT

Please rate the following statements on a scale of 1 to 5, where 1 represents "strongly disagree" and 5 represents "strongly agree."

1	2	3	4	5	The aspects of my life that bring me happiness, fulfillment, and contentment are clear to me.
1	2	3	4	5	I actively seek out new experiences and activities to explore what brings me pleasure.
1	2	3	4	5	I pay attention to my physical, emotional, and mental sensations to identify what brings me pleasure.
1	2	3	4	5	I reflect on past experiences to recognize the circumstances and activities that have given me joy and satisfaction.
1	2	3	4	5	I pursue my passions and interests, as they often bring me pleasure.
1	2	3	4	5	I seek inspiration from various sources like books, podcasts, movies, or art forms to explore different avenues of pleasure.
1	2	3	4	5	I cultivate mindfulness and self-awareness to identify what brings me pleasure.
1	2	3	4	5	I engage in experimentation and communication to better understand my preferences and desires.
1	2	3	4	5	I keep a pleasure journal to document and reflect on moments of joy, pleasure, and fulfillment.
1	2	3	4	5	I am open to seeking professional guidance to further explore my desires and uncover what truly pleases me.

Calculate your average rating: Add up your ratings for all the statements.

Scoring:

40-50 = You have a clear understanding of what brings you pleasure. You know that it is your birthright and you are not afraid to venture out because you realize that discovering new things is what brings you joy. You are confident and don't compromise your morals.

20-29 = You realize that pleasure exist but you have insecurities that you are deserving of it. As a result, you limit your own pleasure and prioritize others. Your morals are on the border of compromise. You deserve to know what it feels like to prioritize you without having to sacrifice moral standards. Continue to discover more of what pleases you and allow it to keep you grounded.

30-39 = You have a great sense of pleasure. You pay attention to your needs and are not afraid to implement change as long as it doesn't make you uncomfortable. You reflect on experiences and use them to help you understand your own pleasure. You embrace the journey but prefer consistency.

1-19 = Pleasure is your birthright! You haven't grasp this concept as yet. You don't feel as if you are deserving of it and you spend little time discovering what makes you happy. You place others needs before your own and you often feel overwhelmed. You compromise your morals often because you don't have a proper foundation of good pleasure.

Conclusion:

I'm so excited that you are putting in the work to understand God's intentions when He created you. He designed you to be able to experience pleasure because He cares. When you truly understand that pleasure is your birthright, it changes how you show up for yourself in this world. You are on a continuous path of discovering you and I'm so proud that you have allowed yourself to experience the process.

⭐ **Disclaimer:**
This assessment is intended for informational and self-reflective purposes only. It is not a substitute for professional counseling, therapy, or advice. Use it as a starting point for self-reflection and personal growth, and be open to adapting your approach as you continue to explore what brings you pleasure. Results should be viewed as a guide and not as a definitive diagnosis or solution. Please consult a qualified professional for personalized support if needed.

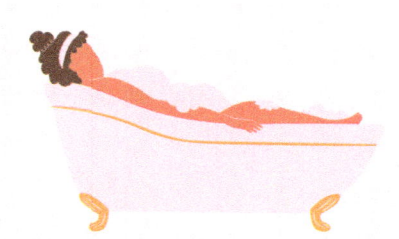

WORD SEARCH

Can you find all the words related to pleasure?

h	s	g	p	s	e	l	f	c	a	r	e	y	l	a
p	l	e	a	s	u	r	e	x	j	t	n	q	d	u
f	o	y	s	i	a	e	n	j	o	y	m	e	n	t
x	v	u	s	o	t	r	p	i	y	t	s	o	g	i
m	e	s	i	h	j	h	a	p	p	i	n	e	s	s
s	s	i	o	u	a	r	t	n	r	e	e	n	a	l
a	l	m	n	k	b	m	s	e	g	r	f	g	g	d
c	b	i	r	t	h	r	i	g	h	t	o	n	e	g
r	i	s	e	n	s	u	a	l	i	t	y	s	e	i
i	d	a	r	e	t	i	n	t	i	m	a	c	y	s
f	e	p	r	i	o	r	i	t	y	s	p	b	i	t
i	a	p	e	a	c	e	u	a	r	o	u	s	a	l
c	n	s	h	j	f	i	d	e	n	t	i	t	y	n
e	u	p	q	w	n	o	i	t	c	a	r	t	t	a
t	f	u	l	f	i	l	l	m	e	n	t	s	e	q

Pleasure	Desire	Selfcare	Priority	Joy
Birthright	Attraction	Enjoyment	Peace	love
Intimacy	Arousal	Happiness	Sacrifice	Fun
Passion	Sensuality	Identity	Fulfillment	One

109

Step workbook Six

Hey God, Help me to overcome my limited beliefs.

Challenge the thoughts and beliefs that hold you back. Replace lies with God's truth and walk in the freedom of a renewed mind.

LET'S CHECK IN

DATE _____

TOP 3 THINGS I WAS INTENTIONAL ABOUT
- _____
- _____
- _____

THIS WEEK I FELT?

WHAT WERE MY PATTERNS?

WHAT DO I NEED TO FOCUS ON NEXT?
_____
_____
_____
_____

WAS I TRIGGERED?

IN WHAT WAY WILL I SHOW UP FOR ME?

MY RANKING OF THE WEEK
☆ ☆ ☆ ☆ ☆

LET'S CREATE A PLAN

MONDAY · TUESDAY · WEDNESDAY

THURSDAY · FRIDAY · SATURDAY

APPOINTMENT TIMES · SUNDAY · TASK/REMINDERS

KEEP GOING!

Misc. doodle

TO-DO'S

PHOTO/reminders?

Just living my best life.

~ STEP 6 ~
HEY GOD, HELP ME TO OVERCOME MY LIMITED BELIEFS.

Affirm - "I give myself permission to evolve!" Ephesians 4:23

1 Samuel 1: 17-18 NIV
"Eli answered, "Go in peace, and may the God of Israel grant you what you have asked of him." She said, "May your servant find favor in your eyes." Then she went her way and ate something, and her face was no longer downcast."

Have you ever wanted something so bad but no matter how hard you tried, it just wasn't happening? Or maybe perhaps something repeatedly kept happening that worked against you? This was the struggle of Hannah. I love this story! Hannah was the first wife of a man by the name of Elkanah. The reason why I say first is because according to scholars, and the culture of the times, Elkanah got another wife because Hannah couldn't get pregnant. During that era, a woman's worth was determined by her ability to conceive. Elkanah loved Hannah so much but he also needed to keep his bloodline alive and that meant by culture, he would sacrifice by securing another wife.

Conflict probably began from the moment Elkanah brought Penninah home. I don't imagine Hannah being super excited that her husband who she loved was having to take a second wife because of her inability to conceive. When Peninnah came, she gave birth again and again. I could only imagine what it must have felt like for Hannah, because she probably felt worthless, like God was punishing her for something. How was it possible for her to love God so much but also feel as though He may have been cursing her. Imagine what it would have been like to go out into town and everyone knowing too much of what's going on in your life, and treating you as if you are cursed. Imagine how many people stopped talking, or mocked her because of it. She probably felt as if she had no one in her corner. She may have felt lonely even though she had a husband who loved her. By nature, I'm sure his attention would be pulled towards the wife with the kids, even if he made an effort to spend time with Hannah. Life could not have been easy for her. Year after year she had to watch her husband with another woman, and interact with children, knowing how badly she wanted to have her own.

Sometimes it has to be just you and God!

Imagine how often she cried, how often she prayed to God not knowing whether or not her desire for kids would ever come true. Year after year, Elkanah would take his family to worship and sacrifice in a town called Shiloh. Could you imagine having to go to a place to give worship to a God you feel is neglecting you. She probably felt as if she had nothing to give. And to add fuel to the fire, it says that during those times, Penninah would torment her. For women who find it difficult to conceive, there is an emptiness that they carry that those who can conceive may not ever understand. There was nothing Elkanah could do to make Hannah's situation better. He would try and give her double portions but she was so consumed by her burden that she probably couldn't appreciate it. I believe he couldn't understand why she wouldn't accept her fate. I believe that he wanted her to accept it. The gesture of him giving her double food meant that it hurt him to see her carry the burden. He wanted her to know that her inability to conceive wasn't a problem for him because he loved her.

It was clear that the issue Hannah had was between she and God, and the torment of Penninah was her fuel. She had to push past her limited beliefs to pray to God in the temple the way she needed to. In the temple, she would pour out her heart in a way that the priest believed Hannah to be drunk. She worshipped God even though she felt like He cursed her. She would lay it all out before God because it was personal. Hannah was tired of her circumstance and feeling the pain of not being able to have a child. Scholars believe that it was a period of nineteen years she dealt with this issue. If this is accurate this would mean that for nineteen years, she dealt with limiting beliefs, that she had to overcome, in order to have a child. What amazes me most about this story was that when Hannah was finally able to conceive, she gave birth to a man that God raised. She dedicated him to the Lord and God used her son Samuel as a prophet and a Priest to call Israel back to a place of repentance.

Hannah didn't know it at the time but her desire to have a child was apart of God's strategic plan. For nineteen years, He groomed her in her tears, her posture, her humility, and her faithfulness. Although it was hard, she trusted God. That final day in the temple after she prayed, she surrendered her will to God and carried on with life as if He answered her prayer, and it was that moment where she conceived.

You may be asking what this story has to do with limiting beliefs. Like Hannah, I'm sure many of you have experienced something that limited what you believe, which is why I urge you to take on the posture of Hannah when the circumstances say otherwise. You are going to have to come to a place where you rise above the Penninah's because what you are carrying is destined for purpose, and you will have to overcome some thoughts to get to the destination. God has given you a certain type of grace because your circumstances have been harder than others.

I need you to believe that you are capable of accomplishing all of your goals, and achieving all that God has destined for you. There are people who are depending on you to deliver them. There are individuals whose destiny is tied to yours. You get to do something out of the ordinary which is why the struggle has been so hard, but this next season of your life is going to require your faith. It is going to require you to go beyond your own thought process and believe.

Hey God,

As I read the story of Hannah, something in me jumped. I struggle in believing that I will have access to the things I desire. I felt like my life has been down for so long that the possibilities of what I want aren't achievable. But the story of Hannah has renewed my hope. Sometimes I want to lose focus because I see other people achieving things and having access to things that I've been praying for. Some of them are not even saved and it can be discouraging, but you have made a promise to me and although it is taking everything in my heart to have this type of faith, I believe you. I believe that I am worthy of success and respect. I believe that I'm growing stronger every day. I believe that every step I take brings me closer to my goals. I believe that I am capable of achieving great things, and I trust the process of growth. I believe that I have the power to create the life I desire, one choice at a time and that growth is a journey, and I am becoming better every day.

In Jesus name!

Activity

Limiting Beliefs Exercise: Reframe and Release

Stage 1: Objective: Identify the Limiting Beliefs.

Instructions:
Write down a recurring negative thought or belief you have about yourself, others, or life.
Use prompts such as:
- "I can't ___ because ___."
- "I'm not ___ enough to ___."
- "People like me don't ___."
- "Success/happiness/pleasure isn't possible for me because ___."

Stage 2: Objective: Reframe the Belief - Replace the limiting belief with an empowering truth.

Instructions: Write a new belief that counters the limiting one.
e.g. "I'm not good enough to succeed."
- Reframed Belief: "I am capable of success, and I am constantly learning and improving."
- Use empowering affirmations that feel authentic and align with your growth.
    - If the Limiting Belief Is: "I'm not strong enough to handle this."
    - Empowering Affirmation: "I am resilient and have everything I need to overcome challenges."

Stage 3: Evaluate the Impact: Identify the Limiting Beliefs - Recognize how this belief is holding you back.

Instructions: Write down:
- "What areas of my life are affected by this belief?"
- "What opportunities have I missed because of this belief?"
- "How does this belief make me feel about myself?"

Stage 4: Challenge the Belief Objective: Deconstruct the belief by questioning its validity.

Instructions: Ask:
- "Is this belief 100% true?"
- "What evidence do I have that contradicts this belief?"
- "What would I say to a friend who had this belief about themselves?"
- Write down answers that reveal why this belief is false, irrational, or outdated.

Stage 5: Reflect on the Origins Objective: Trace the root of the belief to understand where it came from.

Instructions: Ask:
- "Where did this belief come from?"
- "Who told me this, or what experiences reinforced it?"
- "Is this belief based on truth or someone else's opinion?"
- Write your answers to help uncover its origin (e.g., childhood experiences, cultural influences, or past failures).

Activity

Limiting Beliefs Exercise:
Reframe and Release
(Extra writing space)

Stage 1: Objective: Identify the Limiting Beliefs.

Stage 2: Objective: Reframe the Belief – Replace the limiting belief with an empowering truth.

Stage 3: Evaluate the Impact: Identify the Limiting Beliefs – Recognize how this belief is holding you back.

Stage 4: Challenge the Belief Objective: Deconstruct the belief by questioning its validity.

Stage 5: Reflect on the Origins Objective: Trace the root of the belief to understand where it came from.

My Take-away's

1.
2.
3.
4.
5.

DEVOTIONAL NOTES

_____
_____
_____
_____

Top Three Affirmations

★ _____

★ _____

★ _____

Define your goals

▶ _____

▶ _____

▶ _____

▶ _____

▶ _____

▶ _____

▶ _____

▶ _____

▶ _____

▶ _____

▶ _____

▶ _____

▶ _____

Self Care Plans ✓ ✗

1. _____
2. _____
3. _____
4. _____
5. _____
6. _____

Prayer Focus ✓ ✗

1. _____
2. _____
3. _____
4. _____
5. _____
6. _____

Notes

BRAIN DUMP

DATE / /

Hey God, I'm busy a lot! Help me to be intentional.

CLEAR YOUR MIND!
What are all the things I can't stop thinking about?

HIGH PRIORITY
These are my non-negotiables, they have to get done!

LOW PRIORITY
These are important, but can wait.

FREE THOUGHTS
Remember to give yourself grace! You can't be everything to everyone. Fill up your cup and pour from the overflow.

5 Minutes of Meditation

S M T W TH F S

Breathe before writing

INHALE EXHALE INHALE EXHALE INHALE EXHALE

I'm intentionally meditating on?
* _____
* _____
* _____
* _____
* _____

Describe your feelings. You can draw or write.

My Action Step:
_____
_____

Expose meditation lies!

Sometimes, we think about things that are not true. Write down a truth to a lie you heard while meditating and confirm it with a scripture.

Example: I expose the lie that I'm not good enough because God says that I am fearfully and wonderfully made.

This Week's Highlight

Things that you overcame:
_____
_____
_____
_____

"This book of the law shall not depart out of thy mouth; but thou shalt meditate therein day and night." Joshua 1:8

Your mind should be clear. It's time to focus and just write.

Hey God, Can We Talk?   Date:

Your mind should be clear. It's time to focus and just write.

Hey God, Can We Talk?   Date:

Your mind should be clear. It's time to focus and just write.

Hey God, Can We Talk?   Date:

Your mind should be clear. It's time to focus and just write.

Hey God, Can We Talk?   Date:

Your mind should be clear. It's time to focus and just write.

Hey God, Can We Talk? Date:

THE SCRIPTURE THAT KEPT ME ▶

WHAT CAN I DO DIFFERENTLY NEXT TIME?

▶

▶

▶

HOW CAN I REWARD MYSELF?

▶

▶

▶

WHAT WERE MY CHALLENGES? WAS I HARD ON MYSELF? DID I GIVE MYSELF GRACE? HAVE I FORGIVEN MYSELF? LET'S TALK TO GOD ABOUT IT!

Now faith is the substance of things hoped for, the evidence of things not seen Hebrews 11:1 (KJV).

Guided Visualization

Visualize Success!

Record yourself over soft music asking these questions. Play back the recording, close your eyes and meditate your responses. Imagine yourself thriving. Focus on how it feels. Embrace the truth of who you are meant to be. For help, check out the resource at the bottom of the page.

How many children do you have?

How much money is in your bank account?

Whose life is better because of you?

What kind of home are you driving in to?

How much money do you make?

Who is inspiring you?

What kind of job do you have?

Who is thanking you?

Who is living because you decided to not give up?

Do you have a family?

What kind of car are you driving?

How many business calls are you receiving?

Whose life are you changing?

Who is more connected to God because they got a word from you?

Who didn't commit suicide because you showed up?

How does it feel to be used by God?

Do you have a pool?

How many bedrooms do you have?

How does it feel to rest?

Who is sleeping peacefully at night?

How does it feel to not struggle?

Are you afraid of what you see?

How many days do you relax at home with your family?

How does it feel to live in abundance?

How do you feel knowing that you are helping people?

How does it feel to pay your bills on time?

Is this the life you envisioned for yourself?

How does it feel to have stability?

Are you enjoying your family game nights?

How does it feel to ride in first class?

How often are you traveling?

How does it feel to have financial freedom?

How many countries are you visiting?

How many days do you work each week?

How does it feel to be mentally focused?

Who is enjoying this life with you?

How many are on your team?

Mindful Mind. (2024, February 18). GUIDED VISUALIZATION EXERCISE - How to Perform Visualization Correctly. YouTube. https://www.youtube.com/watch?v=r-zXv7aYYqY

Step workbook Seven

Hey God, Help me to understand and pursue purpose?

Discover God's purpose for your life. Reflect on your gifts, passions, and calling, and begin to pursue them with intention.

LET'S CHECK IN

DATE _____

TOP 3 THINGS I WAS INTENTIONAL ABOUT
- ○ _____
- ○ _____
- ○ _____

THIS WEEK I FELT?

WHAT WERE MY PATTERNS?

WHAT DO I NEED TO FOCUS ON NEXT?
_____
_____
_____
_____

WAS I TRIGGERED?

IN WHAT WAY WILL I SHOW UP FOR ME?

MY RANKING OF THE WEEK
☆ ☆ ☆ ☆ ☆

LET'S CREATE A PLAN

MONDAY | TUESDAY | WEDNESDAY

THURSDAY | FRIDAY | SATURDAY

APPOINTMENT TIMES | SUNDAY | TASK/REMINDERS

KEEP GOING!

Misc. doodle

TO DO'S

PHOTO/reminders?

Just living my best life.

~ STEP 7 ~

HEY GOD, HELP ME TO UNDERSTAND AND PURSUE PURPOSE

Affirm: "In order to stop me, they have to stop God!"

Dr. Tiffany R. Harris, Ph.D

2 Kings 4:3-7 NIV
Elisha said, "Go around and ask all your neighbors for empty jars. Don't ask for just a few. Then go inside and shut the door behind you and your sons. Pour oil into all the jars, and as each is filled, put it to one side." She left him and shut the door behind her and her sons. They brought the jars to her and she kept pouring. When all the jars were full, she said to her son, "Bring me another one." But he replied, "There is not a jar left." Then the oil stopped flowing. She went and told the man of God, and he said, "Go, sell the oil and pay your debts. You and your sons can live on what is left."

It was a day in May, 2016 an almost perfect summer day. The weather outside was cooler than usual and I remember heading into my corporate America job thinking there has got to be so much more to my life than just this. I didn't hate the job, but everyday I went to work I felt as though there was more to my life. I knew I was destined for something better. I was working over forty hours a week and still not making enough to afford my bills.

Month after month I struggled and reality would hit, because at that point in my life it had been seven months in a row that the sheriff visited my small two bedroom apartment to put the eviction notice on my door. The notice was my alert to go down to the 3rd floor of the courthouse to ask the judge to give me more time, as my rent accumulated on top of the excessive late fees. I was overwhelmed with debt, and tired but didn't know how to move past the circumstances. I wanted a better life for my daughter.

"You ever thought about Real Estate?" I always wanted to be an agent and I had a mentor who was highly successful in the field. She thought I would be a great agent and I knew if she could do it, why couldn't I right! She became a source that could help me with the process and helped me to get started. I thought if I could get into that field, I would no longer have to sleep at friends' houses because the utilities couldn't get paid. I needed a win and wanted desperately to get out. Every dollar I spent outside of a bill was a sacrifice, but I made a decision to rob Peter to pay Paul. I found a Groupon discount to go to real estate school and paid for it.

You Gotta Keep Going.

I would go to work with my real estate book so I could study while I was on the clock, and head straight to real estate school when I was done. That became my life for the next few weeks.

One day I arrived to my corporate job, real estate book in hand, and before I could sit down at my desk I got a phone call from my sisters boyfriend at the time to inform me that she was being rushed in an ambulance to the hospital. He didn't give me a lot of information other than he had to perform CPR because apparently she wasn't fully breathing. I left work immediately and headed straight to the hospital that they transferred her to. When I arrived they gave me the worst possible diagnosis. She was suffering from not one but two aneurysms. The doctor informed me that they needed to do an emergency brain surgery, and all of a sudden I became the decision maker. They went over all the options and asked me what I would like for them to do. I didn't have time to panic, I had to tell them what I felt she needed based off of the two seconds of information they gave me for her options. That day she went in to have an emergency brain surgery, and my home suddenly became the hospital. Leaving real estate school was not an option, I had to keep going! Instead, I opted to take some paid time off of work. I would eat, sleep and shower at the hospital or spend the night at a friends house who lived nearby on the nights her boyfriend stayed. I would go to real estate school in the evenings and back to her intensive care room and study as I helped the nurses keep an extra eye on her. I would pray, play praise and worship music and study some more.

I remember leaving the hospital one day to do a favor for a friend. I felt like life couldn't get any worse than where it was at that moment. My friend needed me to urgently take her son to a relative who lived nearby. As soon as I got to her home, I called her son to let him know I was outside. I waited on him for five minutes, and when he got into my car, as I was about to reverse, a gentlemen pulled up behind me and blocked me in. I beeped my horn and thought to myself, "Who is this blocking me in?" I was so confused so I put my car in park, got out of the car and approached him. Before I could say anything he asked, "Are you Tamika Bowe?" I responded, "Yes I am , who are you?" He explained that he was from the repossession company and that he came to collect my car. I completely forgot that it had been months that I hadn't made a payment on my car. Truth be told, I had already been hiding my car for several months hoping they wouldn't find me. I was hiding my car for so long, them taking it was not even a thought. I was shocked that they found me at my friends house, so in my mind, they had to have been following me.

This was not going to be a season of walking so I begged and pleaded with the gentlemen to please not take my car away. If I didn't have my car, I wouldn't have been able to go to the hospital or even real estate school. I pleaded with him until he finally said, "If you promise to make your payment I will let you go!" With no money or clue as to how I was going to get it done, I of course told him that I would pay it right away. I couldn't believe he was letting me go. I was desperate and I truthfully wanted to pay

Your current job is your resource.

it, but I was so behind on payments that I just didn't know how or when I could. Unfortunately after dropping my friends son off just when I thought the day couldn't get any worse my car broke down. I sat in the car and took a moment to myself and just cried. I didn't just cry, I screamed. I didn't realize I was holding so much in. I felt like I was in a movie, like my life at the time wasn't real. Surely I couldn't make this up! It had to be make believe. I felt overwhelmed at life and I no longer knew what to do. Should I give up or should I keep going? What do I do? Fortunately, the issue with my car was a simple fix, but it did give me an opportunity to let out the pain I was feeling inside.

After I allowed myself to be realistic about my reality, I had yet another decision to make. This decision was going to impact my future. I had every reason to give up on life because I couldn't see any light at the end of the tunnel. Everything around me was falling apart, and I didn't know how to handle it. I would repeat to myself that the life I was living could not be my real life. I knew that there was so much more to my life, but with everything that was going on, I felt like I had no access. I would see better for my life until the bill couldn't get paid, or I would fall behind, and then the only thing I would see at that point was defeat. There had to be more to life and I had hit rock bottom enough to know that I had been there way too many times. It was a process, my process that I had to go through to prove to myself that there was more to life than just the ground. I would ask God what to do, how do I get out because I was so tired of just living and not enjoying life. It would be a beautiful day outside and the weather would often be perfect, but because so much life was going on around me, the beauty stayed outside. I made a decision that the perception of my reality would change.

During this process of being broke, it broke a lot of things in me. I was allowing my life circumstances to define me, instead of creating the life that was destined for me. It became a consistent cycle of my life on repeat. I became so desperate and wanted change, and ultimately that lead to a bigger purpose. It gave me something to look forward to. I no longer looked at my job as my life, but began looking at it as a resource, or a stepping stool to accomplish something better for myself.

My sister survived and she was able to fully heal and restore, and during the process I never gave up on real estate school. During that season of my life falling apart I managed to keep it together, because I was so desperate to get out of that circumstance. I didn't allow the pressures of life to stop me. It was extremely difficult, but I had to stay focused even though it was difficult to focus. I became a licensed real estate agent and it was a dream come true.

Being an agent wasn't the end goal but I didn't know it at that time. I was able to experience what it meant to be an entrepreneur and that led me into my God given purpose and the career that I am doing today. As an agent I was afforded the opportunity to understand the business world and develop a money growth mindset.

Your current job is your resource.

Elevation comes with consistency and that requires a working system. The system that I created led me to exceeding my own sales goals and selling millions of real estate locally and internationally, and earning consistent income in my businesses. For this weeks devotional, I would like for you to focus on one letter a day and reflect on what it would take to turn your process into purpose.

Day 1. P is to find Purpose in the process - What is it now?

One of the keys to jumpstart your process is to first discover what the process is for. Think about your life and where you are right now. What are you experiencing? What are you tired of? How can you turn what it is you are experiencing into an idea that can bring you income? What are you good at? What comes easy to you without having to think about it? What are you passionate about? If you could do something without getting paid but it still brings you joy, what would that be? Figure out what you are purposed for in the moment. Ask, "What is my why now?"

Discovering the YOU!

Your purpose is tied to your passion and it is typically something you would do even if you weren't getting paid, because it brings you joy and fulfillment. You have to figure out what you are purposed for in the moment, so that you could understand the process. Purpose evolves over time, but there is purpose in the now that needs to be discovered. Proverbs 29:18 - **"Where there is no vision, the people perish."**

You have to be able to see yourself. Write down your personal strengths. For each strength, ask yourself these questions: Ex. Strengths - Communication, creativity, leadership, giving, teaching, active listening, goal setting etc.

- What opportunities are out there for me?
- How could I use this strength more in life or work?
- What distractions do I have?
- How could I turn this strength into an opportunity?
- What ideas have I had that I've been putting off?
- Where could I use this strength to make a difference in my life?
- If life happens, will I let it get in the way of achieving my goals?
- Will I need a backup plan?
- Who will I be serving?

Day 2. A is to Allow your purpose to be your drive.

When I was logging into my corporate job, I knew there was more to life than just the repeat of living to struggle. I hit rock bottom several times before it registered that the ground was not where I was supposed to be. Being a realtor was a way out of poverty and I felt like that was what God was telling me to do at that time. In that season, my purpose drove me. I needed to be an agent and what that required was for me to go to real estate school. Life began hitting me from every direction possible, but because I knew how badly I needed to finish, I couldn't give up. That motivated me to keep going no matter how hard I was hit. My life could no longer be driven by how I felt. That's why I would get up and study for hours at a time even if I didn't feel like it, or not stop because my sister was in the hospital. I didn't give up when the bills would pile up or the distractions would come. I didn't give up because life wasn't going the way I would have desired. What I knew was that I had to get to the end goal, because it meant that my life would change. Working didn't bother me anymore because my perception changed.

My job was no longer depressing because it became the resource that was paying for me to get back and forth to real estate school, and everything else that came with it. My thought process changed because now I was allowing my purpose to drive me to go forward. Drivers are motivators. If you don't have a vision of what your purpose is, you will have no motivation to do anything with purpose in your life.

Create an action plan for setbacks. What kind of tools will you use to ensure that regardless of what happens, you still show up for yourself? **How can being strategic about overcoming obstacles keep you motivated?**

> Habakkuk 2:2-3 "Write the vision, and make it plain upon tables, that he may run that readeth it. For the vision is yet for an appointed time, but at the end it shall speak, and not lie: though it tarry, wait for it; because it will surely come, it will not tarry."

Day 3. I is for It's Inside you!

Begin with what you have. One of my favorite stories in the Bible is the widow woman. She lost her husband and went to the prophet Elisha for help because the creditors had been harassing her. They threatened that if she couldn't pay her debt they would take her children as slaves to cover the debt. As a mother, I couldn't imagine losing my kids because I'm struggling with bills. I feel like if I'm unable to make my car payment, take my car but not my children, or if I can't pay my rent, kick me out but don't take my kids. Unfortunately, that was the norm for that era. If you couldn't pay your debt they had a right to take your children to cover the debt.

The widow woman became desperate and when she went to Elisha, he asked her if there was anything in her home that she could sell. She was in such a bad situation that she didn't focus on what she already had. When he asked her if she had anything at all, her first response was to say no!

The oil was always there! It was there each time they came to collect the debt, but because of her circumstances, she couldn't see it. She had to be desperate enough to see the value of something that was already inside. When she told Elisha she had a little bit of oil, He then gave her the strategy. He told her to borrow as many jars as she could, go home, close the door and pour the little bit of oil in the jars to fill. She didn't question him, she grabbed the jars, and did what Elisha said. There was so much oil that it would not stop flowing. She was able to sell what she had to cover all of her debts, and her family was able to live off the rest.

What are some of the limitations that delay or keep you from moving forward? Who can you borrow jars from? Your neighbors are those who can help you achieve your goals. They include those who can help you with content creation, marketing, systems, budgeting and accounting, social media, or that skill you have been trying to perfect. What this story taught me is that you need an Elisha, (a coach with a strategy) and you can't do it without help and support. (Your neighbors with the jars) It's time to begin searching for a coach and those who can help you accomplish your goals. I want you to always remember that not having one is going to cost you the very thing that is inside of you. It can cost you your children. Think: What coaches and neighbors do I need to help me accomplish my goals? Create a list of those you know with talents and ask them to borrow their jars. This means ask them for help.

Day 4. D is for Desperation Eliminates Fear

If you have come to this point and you still don't know what it is you have that is in you, learn from this woman. What she needed she already had. She just didn't know because she wasn't desperate enough to see it. She was going through the process not knowing what to do, and it wasn't until she met with Elisha that she thought about the oil that she had. What is in you that God can use to multiply to turn into purpose? Is it a book, your voice as a speaker, your knowledge and ability to teach, your experience or your process? Whatever it is, it doesn't take much. God wants you to use what you have. Her business was birthed out of desperation and she was so successful that she had more than enough for her family to live on for the rest of their lives.

If you have not figured out your purpose go read 2 Kings 4:1-7 and meditate on it. Whatever you need to produce income, you already have because it is in you! My virtual coach Eric Thomas would always say, "When you want to succeed more than you want to breathe" the shift in your mindset will begin to change. Find yourself so focused that your purpose becomes the priority.

Your process is preparing you for success, you just haven't discovered it yet. If you don't believe in you then everything you want or desire has already failed. Don't get stuck in the fear component of feeling that if you act on what you see that it will fail. *"What if no one buys the book or shows up to an event? What if no one invests or believes in me? What if no one joins the group or watches the lives?"* This is the thing, all of these are possible scenarios, but what if someone does? What if they buy the book, what if they show up? Your life depends on the beliefs you have and the drive you need to keep going until it does. You have to be able to see the vision without seeing the vision to achieve it. Like the widow woman, if it didn't work out, her children were gone! She didn't have time to think about what may not happen because her faith told her that it had no choice! She had to keep pouring that all until there were no more jars to fill. If you have not reached your goals that means it is not time to stop pouring. Keep pouring until all of your jars are gone.

Day 5 - Create and be consistent while planning

By the time you reach this day you will understand the P.A.I.D. method for your jumpstart. P.A.I.D. is not just an acronym for getting paid; it's about elevating your goals, pursuing purpose, and stepping into a life of passion, alignment, impact, and dedication. In order to be effective with growth, you must create the plan that you desire and just be consistent. God has already given you the tools you need to be successful in your start. You have to believe that you can, so that you will.

What does your process look like so far? Have you discovered purpose in the process? What idea did you come up with to bring to life? Are you desperate enough to push past the fear to execute it? If you can answer all of these questions, you are headed in the write direction.

There will be a lot of challenges when you begin to pursue purpose. The key to the challenge is being prepared and being consistent in showing up. How will you transition when something doesn't work out? Did you have a backup plan or strategy in place? Before you begin, think about your end goal, because it prepares you better for your success, even when things are not working the way you had hoped. Ask yourself a few questions regarding if what you desire has purpose.

- What is the problem that you want to solve with your idea?
- How can your idea bring results to someone else?
- Does your idea relate to your process?
- What is your WHY?

Jeremiah 29:11 "For I know the plans I have for you," declares the Lord, "plans to prosper you and not to harm you, plans to give you hope and a future."

When you can answer these questions, you can communicate clearly your attention to your audience, and begin building that audience to help them with their needs. If you are still struggling with which process, take your time and pray about it. If you have an idea and you're still unsure, try it anyway. You won't know unless you try and if it doesn't work out the first time just try and try again. Don't be afraid to take risk because success requires it. That is the absolute definition of an entrepreneur! On the next page you can begin with a focus chart to help you organize your plan. Remember, your goals should be so big that you have no choice but to rely on God. You are one jumpstart to the beginning of change for your life!

Hey God,

I didn't come this far just to give up. My life experiences have to mean something. Life wasn't just hard because of a desire. It was hard because I had to go through a process to push me to pursue a purpose that was bigger than mine. You reminded me that I was to count it all joy when I go through the fire. You wanted me to find it joy through my pain. You showed me that there was a purpose to live for, and I want to go after it. Thank you for being not just patient, but kind. Thank you for believing in me especially in those times when I didn't have the capacity to believe in myself. You revealed yourself to me in the trials and showed me what I was capable of. Now that I know that I can do it, I won't stop pouring my oil until I do. I will keep pouring. I'm unstoppable because in order to stop me, they would have to stop You!

In Jesus name!

Focus Chart

1

WRITE DOWN THE IDEA

Write all of the ideas you thought about. Notate the strength and weakness of each one. Determine which one you can realistically envision yourself doing.

2

WHAT WOULD IT TAKE?

Research your idea and notate what it would take to accomplish it. Do you need funding? What kind of tools or supplies are needed? How can you solve someones problem with your idea? Are you passionate?

3

CREATE GOALS

Take your research and create goals that you can measure to activate your ideas. What is the realistic timeline you will give yourself to measure your progress?

4

SET TIME ASIDE

Set a schedule so that you can dedicate time aside to work towards your goals. Many individuals have busy schedules including work, kids, families events etc. Schedule what you can so you can execute when you can.

5

FIND SUPPORT

There will be things that can be done on your own but there are also things that require the support of others. Identify task that can be done on your own and separate it from the ones that require assistance. Get help when needed.

6

CONSISTENCY IS KEY

Now that you know what needs to be done it is time to execute it. Begin creating platforms for social media, marketing etc. The goal is to just begin and be consistent no matter what you do. Consistency leads to income!

Get knowledge, Gain insight and Go forward!

142

My Take-away's

1.
2.
3.
4.
5.

DEVOTIONAL NOTES

_____
_____
_____
_____

Top Three Affirmations

★ _____

★ _____

★ _____

Define your goals

▶ _____

▶ _____

▶ _____

▶ _____

▶ _____

▶ _____

▶ _____

▶ _____

▶ _____

▶ _____

▶ _____

▶ _____

▶ _____

Self Care Plans ✅ ❌

1. _____ ____
2. _____ ____
3. _____ ____
4. _____ ____
5. _____ ____
6. _____ ____

Prayer Focus ✅ ❌

1. _____ ____
2. _____ ____
3. _____ ____
4. _____ ____
5. _____ ____
6. _____ ____

Notes

BRAIN DUMP

DATE / /

Hey God, I'm busy a lot! Help me to be intentional.

CLEAR YOUR MIND!
What are all the things I can't stop thinking about?

HIGH PRIORITY
These are my non-negotiables, they have to get done!

LOW PRIORITY
These are important, but can wait.

FREE THOUGHTS
Remember to give yourself grace! You can't be everything to everyone. Fill up your cup and pour from the overflow.

5 Minutes of Meditation

S M T W TH F S

Breathe before writing

INHALE EXHALE INHALE EXHALE INHALE EXHALE

I'm intentionally meditating on?

* _____
* _____
* _____
* _____
* _____

Describe your feelings. You can draw or write.

My Action Step:
_____
_____

Expose meditation lies!

Sometimes, we think about things that are not true. Write down a truth to a lie you heard while meditating and confirm it with a scripture.

Example: I expose the lie that I'm not good enough because God says that I am fearfully and wonderfully made.

This Week's Highlight

Things that you overcame:
_____
_____
_____
_____

"This book of the law shall not depart out of thy mouth; but thou shalt meditate therein day and night." Joshua 1:8

Your mind should be clear. It's time to focus and just write.

Hey God, Can We Talk?   Date:

Your mind should be clear. It's time to focus and just write.

Hey God, Can We Talk?   Date:

Your mind should be clear. It's time to focus and just write.

Hey God, Can We Talk?   Date:

Your mind should be clear. It's time to focus and just write.

Hey God, Can We Talk? Date:

Your mind should be clear. It's time to focus and just write.

Hey God, Can We Talk? Date:

THE SCRIPTURE THAT KEPT ME ▶

WHAT CAN I DO DIFFERENTLY NEXT TIME?

▶

▶

▶

HOW CAN I REWARD MYSELF?

▶

▶

▶

WHAT WERE MY CHALLENGES? WAS I HARD ON MYSELF? DID I GIVE MYSELF GRACE? HAVE I FORGIVEN MYSELF? LET'S TALK TO GOD ABOUT IT!

CAN YOU COMPLETE THE PURPOSE CROSSWORD PUZZLE?

Can you find the best word that matches the scripture relating to purpose?

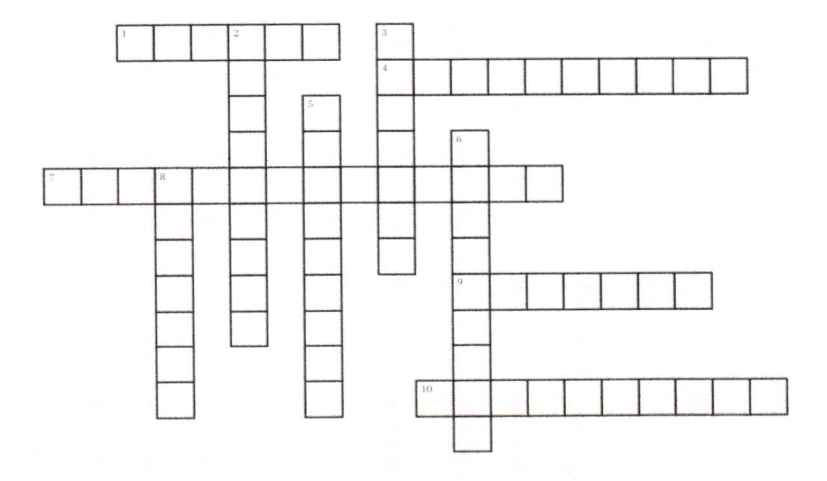

Down:

2. Proverbs 19:21 (NIV): - "Many are the plans in a person's heart, but it is the Lord's purpose that prevails."

3. Colossians 3:23 (NIV) :- "Whatever you do, work at it with all your heart, as working for the Lord..."

5. Amos 3:3 (NIV): "Do two walk together unless they have agreed to do so?"

6. Proverbs 3:6 (NIV): "In all your ways submit to him, and he will make your paths straight."

8. Jeremiah 29:11 - "For I know the plans I have for you," declares the Lord, "plans to prosper you and not to harm you, plans to give you hope and a future."

Across:

1. Proverbs 29:18 (KJV): "Where there is no vision, the people perish."

4. Philippians 3:14 (NIV): "I press on toward the goal to win the prize for which God has called me heavenward in Christ Jesus."

7. Galatians 6:5 (NIV): "For each one should carry their own load."

9. 2 Timothy 1:9 (NIV): "He has saved us and called us to a holy life—not because of anything we have done but because of his own purpose..."

10. Proverbs 16:3 - "Commit to the Lord whatever you do, and he will establish your plans."

Word Bank:
Intention, Calling, Alignment, Aspiration, Direction, Purpose
Vision, Responsibility, Passion, Commitment

ANSWER KEY: 1.Vision, 2.Intention, 3.Passion, 4.Aspiration, 5.Alignment, 6.Direction, 7.Responsibilty, 8.Purpose, 9.Calling, 10.Commitment

Step
workbook Eight

Hey God, Help me to trust the process.

Lean into faith and patience. Learn to trust God's timing and His work in your life, even when you don't see the full picture.

LET'S CHECK IN

DATE _____

TOP 3 THINGS I WAS INTENTIONAL ABOUT
- _____
- _____
- _____

THIS WEEK I FELT?

WHAT WERE MY PATTERNS?

WHAT DO I NEED TO FOCUS ON NEXT?
_____
_____
_____
_____

WAS I TRIGGERED?

IN WHAT WAY WILL I SHOW UP FOR ME?

MY RANKING OF THE WEEK
☆ ☆ ☆ ☆ ☆

LET'S CREATE A PLAN

MONDAY　　　　　TUESDAY　　　　　WEDNESDAY

THURSDAY　　　　　FRIDAY　　　　　SATURDAY

APPOINTMENT TIMES　　　SUNDAY　　　TASK/REMINDERS

KEEP GOING!

Misc. doodle

TO-DO'S

PHOTO/reminders?

Just living my best life.

~ STEP 8 ~

HEY GOD, HELP ME TO TRUST THE PROCESS.

Affirm - "I have been called for such a time as this!" Esther 4:14

Esther 4:14 NIV
"And who knows but that you have come to your royal position for such a time as this?"

The word "process" has always been a source of discomfort for me. I didn't grasp the true meaning of the word until I experienced several different processes in my life. Being uncomfortable was never something I enjoyed. Yet, that's exactly what a process does—it pushes you out of your comfort zone. Process is uncomfortable but necessary for growth. I wouldn't be who I am today without growing through something. I wouldn't have been able to write this book if I didn't learn a thing or two.

"Process" is God's way of refining us, preparing us, and positioning us to fulfill His plans. It often involves waiting patiently, trusting, learning, and stepping out in faith. It's not about rushing the outcome but embracing each step as an opportunity for growth and transformation, which is why I love the story of Esther. At a young age, she lost both of her parents and was raised by her cousin Mordecai. I'm sure that couldn't have been easy for her. Growing up without her parents likely brought feelings of grief, loss, and insecurity. Yet, it may have also strengthened her resilience and dependence on God. Mordecai became both her guardian and spiritual mentor. His guidance instilled values in her like faithfulness, humility, and courage in spite of her circumstances. I believe that he was a great influence and teacher to her which is why she trusted him. This lead to a very necessary journey once she entered the palace and was chosen to be the wife of the King. Her "process" saved an entire genealogy of people.

For this devotional, I want to talk a little bit about Esther's process to help you to understand your own. Read the book of Esther, and for the activity, spend each day this week reflecting on the questions given and journal your reflections.

1. Process is preparation that feels unnecessary

Esther's journey began with humble and painful beginnings as an orphan raised by her cousin Mordecai. Living in exile as a Jew in Persia, she likely experienced loss, uncertainty, and a sense of being overlooked. When the decree went out to gather young women for the king's selection process, Esther's inclusion was a random opportunity. Yet, her year-long beauty treatments and separation from her familiar life, symbolized the unseen preparation God was doing in her heart and character for a greater purpose.

Ask yourself, "How can I trust that the challenges and uncomfortable seasons in my life are part of God's preparation for something greater?"

2. Process births Humility and Strength

As Esther entered the palace, she distinguished herself not by wealth or status, but through her humility, grace, and quiet strength. She took Mordecai's advice to keep her Jewish identity hidden and gained the favor of Hegai, the eunuch in charge of the women. While other women probably relied on outward appearances, Esther's humility and teachability won her favor with everyone she encountered, preparing her for the challenges ahead.

Ask yourself, "How have past disadvantages or missed opportunities shaped my character, and how can humility and strength help me embrace the opportunities that God places before me?"

3. Process builds character

Becoming queen was not the end of Esther's journey but the beginning of her refinement. Her character was tested when Mordecai found out there was a plot to kill the king as Haman orchestrated a plan to destroy the Jews. In the face of these circumstances, Esther demonstrated patience, discernment, and courage. The process revealed her ability to balance wisdom with boldness, showing that leadership requires more than position—it demands a steadfast and godly character.

Ask yourself, "What challenges in my life are shaping my character right now, and how can I embrace them?"

4. Process leads to purpose

Esther's purpose came into focus when Mordecai challenged her with the famous words, "Who knows but that you have come to your royal position for such a time as this?" (Esther 4:14). Her placement in the palace, her favor with the king, and her position as queen were not coincidental but divinely orchestrated. It became clear that she was chosen to act as a mediator for her people, stepping into a purpose that was far greater than herself.

Ask yourself, "How can I discern and step into the unique purpose God has prepared for me, even if it feels intimidating or unclear?" Bonus ask; "Who will lose, if I don't pursue my purpose?"

5. Process Involves Trust and Surrender

Esther's decision to approach the king uninvited required complete trust in God and surrender to His will. Knowing it could cost her life, she fasted and prayed for three days, along with all the other Jews. Her words, "**If I perish, I perish**" (Esther 4:16), reflected her ultimate surrender to God's plan. This step of faith marked a turning point, as she chose to rely on God's strength rather than her own understanding or abilities.

Ask yourself, "What areas of my life require me to surrender control and fully trust God's plan, even when the outcome is uncertain?"

6. Process is a Transformational Journey

Throughout her journey, Esther transformed from a passive young woman into a courageous leader who stood boldly for her people. She carefully strategized her approach to the king and exposed Haman's plot, balancing wisdom, patience, and boldness. The process not only revealed her strength but also deepened her faith and dependence on God, transforming her into the woman God called her to be.

Ask yourself, "How has God transformed me through the process I've experienced so far, and how can I remain open to further growth?"

7. Breakthrough: The Fulfillment of the Process

Esther's process reached its highest when she successfully petitioned the king, leading to Haman's fall and the deliverance of the Jewish people. Her courage saved an entire nation, and Mordecai was elevated to a position of honor. Esther's story demonstrates that the fulfillment of the process is not just personal victory—it's about fulfilling God's greater purpose, bringing restoration, justice, and blessings to others.

Ask yourself, "How can I use the breakthroughs and victories in my life to bring blessings and restoration to others, just as Esther did?"

> Prayer:
> Hey God, thank you for allowing me to go through a process that will refine me. Although many times it seems that some of the things in life I experience are unnecessary, you have showed me that everything that I experience is for such a time as this. Continue to give me the strength to be able to press like Esther because I believe that there is something greater on the other side of this and I couldn't thank you enough for choosing me to go through it because I know that the end result is more than just about me.
> In Jesus name!

My Take-away's

1.
2.
3.
4.
5.

DEVOTIONAL NOTES

Top Three Affirmations

★ _____
★ _____
★ _____

Define your goals

▸ _____
▸ _____
▸ _____
▸ _____
▸ _____
▸ _____
▸ _____
▸ _____
▸ _____
▸ _____
▸ _____
▸ _____

Self Care Plans ✅ ❎

1. _____
2. _____
3. _____
4. _____
5. _____
6. _____

Prayer Focus ✅ ❎

1. _____
2. _____
3. _____
4. _____
5. _____
6. _____

Notes

BRAIN DUMP

DATE / /

Hey God, I'm busy a lot! Help me to be intentional.

CLEAR YOUR MIND!
What are all the things I can't stop thinking about?

HIGH PRIORITY
These are my non-negotiables, they have to get done!

LOW PRIORITY
These are important, but can wait.

FREE THOUGHTS
Remember to give yourself grace! You can't be everything to everyone. Fill up your cup and pour from the overflow.

5 Minutes of Meditation

S M T W TH F S

Breathe before writing

INHALE EXHALE INHALE EXHALE INHALE EXHALE

I'm intentionally meditating on?

* _____
* _____
* _____
* _____
* _____

Describe your feelings. You can draw or write.

My Action Step:
_____
_____

Expose meditation lies!

Sometimes, we think about things that are not true. Write down a truth to a lie you heard while meditating and confirm it with a scripture.

Example: I expose the lie that I'm not good enough because God says that I am fearfully and wonderfully made.

This Week's Highlight

Things that you overcame:
_____
_____
_____
_____

"This book of the law shall not depart out of thy mouth; but thou shalt meditate therein day and night." Joshua 1:8

Your mind should be clear. It's time to focus and just write.

Hey God, Can We Talk?   Date:

Your mind should be clear. It's time to focus and just write.

Hey God, Can We Talk?   Date:

Your mind should be clear. It's time to focus and just write.

Hey God, Can We Talk?   Date:

Your mind should be clear. It's time to focus and just write.

Hey God, Can We Talk?   Date:

Your mind should be clear. It's time to focus and just write.

Hey God, Can We Talk? Date:

THE SCRIPTURE THAT KEPT ME ▶

WHAT CAN I DO DIFFERENTLY NEXT TIME?

▶

▶

▶

HOW CAN I REWARD MYSELF?

▶

▶

▶

WHAT WERE MY CHALLENGES? WAS I HARD ON MYSELF? DID I GIVE MYSELF GRACE? HAVE I FORGIVEN MYSELF? LET'S TALK TO GOD ABOUT IT!

"I HAVE BEEN CALLED FOR SUCH A TIME AS THIS!"

Esther 4:14

Step workbook Nine

Hey God, Help me to stay aligned with my goals.

Set goals that align with God's purpose for you. Reflect on how to balance spiritual, personal, and practical priorities.

LET'S CHECK IN

DATE _____

TOP 3 THINGS I WAS INTENTIONAL ABOUT
- ○ _____
- ○ _____
- ○ _____

WHAT WERE MY PATTERNS?

THIS WEEK I FELT?

WHAT DO I NEED TO FOCUS ON NEXT?
_____
_____
_____
_____

WAS I TRIGGERED?

IN WHAT WAY WILL I SHOW UP FOR ME?

MY RANKING OF THE WEEK
☆ ☆ ☆ ☆ ☆

LET'S CREATE A PLAN

MONDAY　　　　　　TUESDAY　　　　　　WEDNESDAY

THURSDAY　　　　　　FRIDAY　　　　　　SATURDAY

APPOINTMENT TIMES　　　SUNDAY　　　TASK/REMINDERS

KEEP GOING!

Misc. doodle

TO-DO'S

PHOTO/reminders?

Just living my best life.

~ STEP 9 ~

HEY GOD, HELP ME TO STAY ALIGNED WITH MY GOALS.

Affirm - ""I am focused, disciplined, and guided by God's wisdom as I pursue my goals. My plans align with His purpose, and I trust Him to establish my steps."

John 4:13-14 NIV
"Jesus answered, "Everyone who drinks this water will be thirsty again, 14 but whoever drinks the water I give them will never thirst. Indeed, the water I give them will become in them a spring of water welling up to eternal life."

I went back and forth about using this scripture to pursue goals but as I read the story of the Samaritan, I thought that it was so profound. In the story of the Samaritan woman at the well, drawing water from the well wasn't just a simple task—it was part of her daily life and survival. In the context of that time and place, water was a crucial resource for daily living, and women typically went to wells to gather it for their households.

For the Samaritan woman, drawing water from the well symbolized a routine task that she had to perform every day, but it also represented something deeper in her life:

1. **A Necessity for Survival:** Water was essential for drinking, cooking, cleaning, and all other aspects of life in a desert region. The goal of drawing water, therefore, was about fulfilling a fundamental need.
2. **The Source of Her Identity and Reputation:** This task was linked to her status in society. She went to the well at a time when she was likely avoiding other women, who may have judged her for her past and multiple marriages. This illustrates how the routine task of drawing water became connected to her emotional and social life.
3. **An Ordinary Act with Greater Significance:** When Jesus approached her and offered "living water," He invited her to think beyond the physical task of drawing water. The physical need for water represented a deeper, spiritual thirst that only Jesus could fulfill. So, her "goal" of drawing water took on a new meaning as Jesus offered her something far more valuable: eternal life and healing for her soul. In this sense, her goal of drawing water symbolized

Goals help you to stay aligned

both the ordinary, necessary aspects of life and the deeper, spiritual longing she had for something more—something only Jesus could provide. This is why her encounter at the well became a pivotal moment of transformation. Oftentimes we take simple goals for granted but for the Samaritan woman, she had to be intentional about creating goals to draw water because that simple goal aligned her with a bigger purpose.

As the saying goes, "If you fail to plan, you plan to fail!" Goal setting is important because it provides direction, focus, and motivation in life. It helps you clarify what you want to achieve, break it into actionable steps, and measure your progress along the way. Here's why it matters:

1. **Provides Clarity and Focus** - The Samaritan woman wanted to keep a low profile and simply fulfill her daily task without drawing attention to her personal life. I believe this was a coping mechanism shaped by her past and social circumstances but who would have known that this goal would have led to her encounter with Jesus. Goals give you a clear sense of purpose and direction. They help you prioritize what's truly important and avoid distractions.

2. **Motivates and Inspires Action** - One encounter with Jesus shifted her goal to purpose. She was no longer defined by her past mistakes or social rejection. Jesus acknowledged her truth without condemnation, offering her grace and acceptance. This transformed her understanding of her worth and shifted her focus from hiding her past to embracing her future in God's plan in which she testified to others. Having goals energizes you to take action and pushes you to strive for improvement. It creates a sense of excitement and determination.

3. **Helps Measure Progress** - The impact of her testimony was evident in how many people from her town came to believe in Jesus, showing her that her efforts were bearing fruit. I believe it was in the freedom of not having to hide any longer. Setting goals allows you to track your progress and celebrate milestones, which keeps you motivated and aware of how far you've come.

4. **Builds Confidence and Discipline** - Despite her past, she boldly shared her story with confidence, showing a newfound discipline in stepping into her purpose and speaking about Jesus. Achieving goals boosts self-esteem and reinforces the belief that you are capable. It also instills discipline as you work toward your objectives.

5. **Encourages Growth and Learning** - Her encounter with Jesus challenged her to grow spiritually and to understand deeper truths about worship and God's plan, transforming her perspective and priorities. The process of pursuing goals challenges you to grow, adapt, and develop new skills. Even setbacks become opportunities to learn.

6. **Aligns with Purpose and Vision** - Through her actions, the Samaritan woman aligned her life with God's vision for her—to be a vessel of His truth and a catalyst for transformation in her community. Goals ensure that your daily actions align with your long-term vision and values, helping you live a more intentional and purpose-filled life.

By setting goals, you take charge of your life and create a roadmap to turn dreams into reality. Her story reminds us that even in brokenness, clear goals aligned with God's will can lead to profound purpose and transformation.

Hey God,

Goal setting isn't new to me but it hasn't been an area of strength. I've always been told about how I should create goals but I never really understood how significant it was until I related it to the lady at the well. It's amazing how setting small goals can achieve things that I haven't even thought about. I want to be better at disciplining myself to create goals. I desire to create goals that align with the purpose you have for my life. Help me to be more intentional with goal setting and planning. Help me to avoid distractions and plan for things that I can control. Help me to not get discouraged from all the things that are beyond my control because I know that you have a way of working out even the smallest details. Help me to be consistent so that I can measure my progress. Thank you for giving me the confidence and inspiring me to make change in my life. Because of you, I know that by making small changes in the way that I do things will push me into being more intentional about goals.

In Jesus name!

Activity

The Goal Climber

What to do: Use the below steps to write your ultimate goal.
Use each step to outline smaller steps toward achieving it.
Why it's fun: It breaks goals into manageable steps and provides a visual roadmap.
For ex: If your ultimate goal is to lose 20 lbs., what are all the steps you would need to accomplish in order to reach your ideal weight loss? A step could be join the gym, go 2 to 3 times a week, create a healthy diet plan etc...

Ultimate Goal:

My Take-away's

1.
2.
3.
4.
5.

DEVOTIONAL NOTES

_____
_____
_____
_____

Top Three Affirmations

★ _____
★ _____
★ _____

Define your goals

▶ _____
▶ _____
▶ _____
▶ _____
▶ _____
▶ _____
▶ _____
▶ _____
▶ _____
▶ _____
▶ _____
▶ _____
▶ _____

Self Care Plans ✅ ❌

1. _____
2. _____
3. _____
4. _____
5. _____
6. _____

Prayer Focus ✅ ❌

1. _____
2. _____
3. _____
4. _____
5. _____
6. _____

Notes

BRAIN DUMP

DATE / /

Hey God, I'm busy a lot! Help me to be intentional.

CLEAR YOUR MIND!
What are all the things I can't stop thinking about?

HIGH PRIORITY
These are my non-negotiables, they have to get done!

LOW PRIORITY
These are important, but can wait.

FREE THOUGHTS
Remember to give yourself grace! You can't be everything to everyone. Fill up your cup and pour from the overflow.

5 Minutes of Meditation

S M T W TH F S

Breathe before writing

INHALE EXHALE INHALE EXHALE INHALE EXHALE

I'm intentionally meditating on?

* _____
* _____
* _____
* _____
* _____

Describe your feelings. You can draw or write.

My Action Step:

_____
_____

Expose meditation lies!

Sometimes, we think about things that are not true. Write down a truth to a lie you heard while meditating and confirm it with a scripture.

Example: I expose the lie that I'm not good enough because God says that I am fearfully and wonderfully made.

This Week's Highlight

Things that you overcame:

_____
_____
_____
_____

"This book of the law shall not depart out of thy mouth; but thou shalt meditate therein day and night." Joshua 1:8

Your mind should be clear. It's time to focus and just write.

Hey God, Can We Talk? Date:

Your mind should be clear. It's time to focus and just write.

Hey God, Can We Talk?   Date:

Your mind should be clear. It's time to focus and just write.

Hey God, Can We Talk?   Date:

Your mind should be clear. It's time to focus and just write.

Hey God, Can We Talk?   Date:

Your mind should be clear. It's time to focus and just write.

Hey God, Can We Talk?   Date:

THE SCRIPTURE THAT KEPT ME ▶

WHAT CAN I DO DIFFERENTLY NEXT TIME?

▶

▶

▶

HOW CAN I REWARD MYSELF?

▶

▶

▶

WHAT WERE MY CHALLENGES? WAS I HARD ON MYSELF? DID I GIVE MYSELF GRACE? HAVE I FORGIVEN MYSELF? LET'S TALK TO GOD ABOUT IT!

RATE YOUR

GOAL SETTING

SELF-AWARENESS AND CONFIDENCE IN DIFFERENT AREAS OF GOAL SETTING. RATE YOURSELF BETWEEN 1 (LOW) AND 10 (HIGH) IN EACH CATEGORY:

CLARITY OF GOALS
HOW CLEAR AND SPECIFIC ARE YOUR GOALS?

1   2   3   4   5   6   7   8   9   10

NOT VERY   EXTREMELY

PLANNING AND ORGANIZATION
HOW WELL DO YOU PLAN AND ORGANIZE THE STEPS TO ACHIEVE YOUR GOALS?

1   2   3   4   5   6   7   8   9   10

NOT VERY   EXTREMELY

MOTIVATION AND DRIVE
HOW MOTIVATED AND DETERMINED ARE YOU TO PURSUE YOUR GOALS?

1   2   3   4   5   6   7   8   9   10

NOT VERY   EXTREMELY

ADAPTABILITY
HOW WELL DO YOU ADJUST TO SETBACKS OR CHANGES IN YOUR GOALS?

1   2   3   4   5   6   7   8   9   10

NOT VERY   EXTREMELY

ABILITY TO STICK TO GOALS
HOW EFFECTIVELY DO YOU TRACK PROGRESS AND HOLD YOURSELF ACCOUNTABLE?

1   2   3   4   5   6   7   8   9   10

NOT VERY   EXTREMELY

Step workbook Ten

Hey God, Help me to create habits for success.

Develop consistent habits that lead to spiritual, emotional, and practical growth. Learn to build a lifestyle that supports your transformation.

This Month, I Declare That:

DECLARATIONS

1. I will trust in the Lord with all my heart and lean not on my own understanding (Proverbs 3:5).
2. The Lord will direct my steps, and I will walk in His perfect will (Proverbs 16:9).
3. God's grace is sufficient for me, and His strength is made perfect in my weakness (2 Corinthians 12:9).
4. I am planted by streams of living water, and I will bear fruit in every season (Psalm 1:3).
5. I will not grow weary in doing good, for in due time I will reap a harvest (Galatians 6:9).
6. The Lord will supply all my needs according to His riches in glory (Philippians 4:19).
7. I will delight myself in the Lord, and He will give me the desires of my heart (Psalm 37:4).
8. God is my refuge and strength, and I will not fear any storm (Psalm 46:1-2).
9. I will be still and know that He is God, trusting in His power and sovereignty (Psalm 46:10).
10. I am blessed in the city and blessed in the field; God's blessings will overtake me (Deuteronomy 28:3-6).
11. The Lord will fight for me, and I will stand firm in His promises (Exodus 14:14).
12. I will cast all my cares on the Lord, for He cares for me deeply (1 Peter 5:7).
13. I will sow seeds of righteousness and reap a harvest of joy and peace (Hosea 10:12).
14. God will make all grace abound to me, so I will abound in every good work (2 Corinthians 9:8).
15. The Spirit of God is upon me, and I am anointed to fulfill His purpose (Isaiah 61:1).

Goals

This month, I declare that my life is aligned with God's Word, my heart is filled with His joy, and I will walk in the fullness of His promises! ✨🙏

LET'S CHECK IN

DATE _____

TOP 3 THINGS I WAS INTENTIONAL ABOUT
- ○ _____
- ○ _____
- ○ _____

THIS WEEK I FELT?

WHAT WERE MY PATTERNS?

WHAT DO I NEED TO FOCUS ON NEXT?
_____
_____
_____
_____

WAS I TRIGGERED?

IN WHAT WAY WILL I SHOW UP FOR ME?

MY RANKING OF THE WEEK
☆ ☆ ☆ ☆ ☆

LET'S CREATE A PLAN

MONDAY

TUESDAY

WEDNESDAY

THURSDAY

FRIDAY

SATURDAY

APPOINTMENT TIMES

SUNDAY

TASK/REMINDERS

KEEP GOING!

Misc. doodle

TO-DO'S

PHOTO/reminders?

Just living my best life.

~ STEP 10 ~

HEY GOD, HELP ME TO CREATE HABITS FOR SUCCESS.

Affirm - "Great things are ahead of me!"

Ruth 1:20-21 NIV
"Don't call me Naomi," she told them. "Call me Mara, because the Almighty has made my life very bitter. I went away full, but the Lord has brought me back empty. Why call me Naomi? The Lord has afflicted me; the Almighty has brought misfortune upon me."

Success is intentional. There are very few who would testify that their success was an accident. I make it a point to attend motivational and business development conferences. No matter how many millionaires I'm surrounded by, I'm amazed because they are sitting at the same conference I'm at getting the same information that I'm getting. Regardless of how many millions are in attendance, they are all showing up, being intentional about their success. Why? Because it doesn't happen by accident.

You are in a position where you have discovered that there is a version of yourself worth knowing. So far up to this point, you have been intentional in understanding that you are enough. You have dealt with some of your pain points and can see yourself as the image of God. You are in a season of fixing broken pieces and putting them together again. You are understanding that God wants you to live a purpose-filled life in mind, body and spirit, and that includes your ability to access pleasure. I know some days might be hard because of the limited beliefs, but now you understand your purpose and are on a path to pursue it. Finally you are grasping the concepts of showing up for yourself because you are realizing that to be successful requires that you move with intention.

Many don't accomplish success because you can't become successful without creating a habit. This means being like Ruth and Naomi, creating plans that align with purpose. You have to start thinking, acting and moving in a direction of success even if you don't understand what that means.

Habits lead to Success.

Stop operating in fear and replace that fear with knowledge to give you the confidence to move in the direction that leads to success. Naomi, her husband Elimelech, and their two sons moved from Bethlehem to Moab to escape a famine. When she and her family initially left, it was because life was so difficult they needed to go where they could survive. The irony is that she lost her husband and her sons and after they died, she learned that the famine had ended. Maybe they could have stayed in Bethlehem and ride out the storm but they were so poor at the time that they did what was necessary. When they died, as a wife and a mother would, Naomi felt bitter, and abandoned by God. Naomi interpreted her suffering as a direct act of God's judgment or discipline towards her. Her words, "The Almighty has brought misfortune upon me," showed that she believed God had turned against her. I believe having her daughter in love, Ruth, gave her some strength to keep fighting in the midst of poverty.

Success is not going to always feel good. Sometimes you will feel hopeless which is why created habits are important. Creating habits develops a routine so that regardless of what goes on in your life, there is a system in place to keep you going. Here's how Ruth created habits for success:

1. Ruth Built a Habit of Loyalty and Commitment
- Success Habit: She prioritized relationships over convenience, she didn't know what was on the other side of Naomi but her character made Ruth trust her. Loyalty to people and values often creates opportunities for long-term growth.

2. Ruth Took Initiative and Was Proactive
- Success Habit: Ruth didn't wait for opportunities, she created a habit of taking initiative and showed her willingness to work hard and seize opportunities, even in difficult circumstances. You can't rely on others to push you. You have to take initiative and be proactive for the future you desire.

3. Ruth Practiced Diligence and Perseverance
- Success Habit: She demonstrated a habit of perseverance and consistency, which earned her recognition and favor because she worked tirelessly in Boaz's fields. When you constantly show up, it attracts others because they see you.

4. Ruth Listened to Wise Counsel
- Success Habit: By making it a habit to listen to "Coach" Naomi, Ruth positioned herself for success and opened doors that would have otherwise remained closed. Having a coach or mentor positions you.

5. Ruth Demonstrated Humility and Gratitude
- Success Habit: Her habit of humility and thankfulness cultivated goodwill, ensuring she was remembered for her character. Starting small is okay. Eventually if you are consistent there will be elevated growth.

6. Ruth Focused on Service
- Success Habit: She developed the habit of serving others, which allowed her to build meaningful relationships and achieve shared success. Serving allows opportunities to gain favor with others.

7. Ruth Maintained Faith in God's Plan
- Success Habit: She aligned her faith to "Naomi's" God, which enabled her to act with hope and purpose. Having faith paves the way for greater purpose.

Ruth's habits of loyalty, hard work, humility, perseverance, gratitude, and faith created a foundation for her success. They led her to Boaz, whose marriage to her restored Naomi's family line and positioned Ruth as the great-grandmother of King David, part of Jesus' lineage. Ruth's story teaches us that success is often the result of consistent, character-driven habits, coupled with faith and action.

Prayer:

Hey God, I want to be able to create habits that lead to success. I understand that in order for me to get to a different place in my life, I must be intentional. I don't want to repeat the same mistakes and do the same wrong things over and over again. I recognize that I can't do this on my own. I can't accomplish what I want to accomplish without soliciting your help. I ask that in this season that you teach me how to create habits that are necessary for my growth. Align me with people who are attached to my destiny. Connect me with destiny helpers and mentors who can give me guidance and teach me when I'm doing something wrong. I don't want to be in this position anymore. I desire to walk in your abundance and live the life that you have destined for me.

In Jesus name!

Activity
Social Media Challenge (Accountability)

- Use the below to write down a list of habits you would like to create, check when completed and discuss what you got from it.
- Create a social media accountability group or use a hashtag for your habit-building journey.
- Share updates, photos, or short videos each day showing how you're working on your goals. Seeing others join the challenge can motivate you to stay on track and make it more fun to stay consistent.

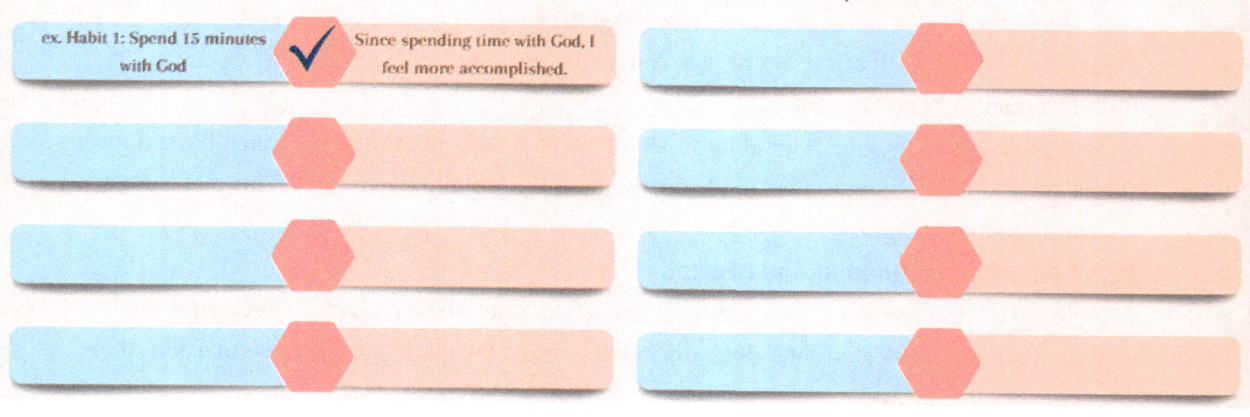

ex. Habit 1: Spend 15 minutes with God ✓	Since spending time with God, I feel more accomplished.		

My Take-away's

1.
2.
3.
4.
5.

DEVOTIONAL NOTES

Top Three Affirmations

★ _____
★ _____
★ _____

Define your goals

▶ _____
▶ _____
▶ _____
▶ _____
▶ _____
▶ _____
▶ _____
▶ _____
▶ _____
▶ _____
▶ _____
▶ _____
▶ _____

Self Care Plans ✅ ❌

1. _____
2. _____
3. _____
4. _____
5. _____
6. _____

Prayer Focus ✅ ❌

1. _____
2. _____
3. _____
4. _____
5. _____
6. _____

Notes

BRAIN DUMP

DATE / /

Hey God, I'm busy a lot! Help me to be intentional.

CLEAR YOUR MIND!
What are all the things I can't stop thinking about?

HIGH PRIORITY
These are my non-negotiables, they have to get done!

LOW PRIORITY
These are important, but can wait.

FREE THOUGHTS
Remember to give yourself grace! You can't be everything to everyone. Fill up your cup and pour from the overflow.

5 Minutes of Meditation

S M T W TH F S

Breathe before writing

INHALE EXHALE INHALE EXHALE INHALE EXHALE

I'm intentionally meditating on?

* _____
* _____
* _____
* _____
* _____

Describe your feelings. You can draw or write.

My Action Step:
_____
_____

Expose meditation lies!

Sometimes, we think about things that are not true. Write down a truth to a lie you heard while meditating and confirm it with a scripture.

Example: I expose the lie that I'm not good enough because God says that I am fearfully and wonderfully made.

This Week's Highlight

Things that you overcame:
_____
_____
_____
_____

"This book of the law shall not depart out of thy mouth; but thou shalt meditate therein day and night." Joshua 1:8

Your mind should be clear. It's time to focus and just write.

Hey God, Can We Talk?   Date:

Your mind should be clear. It's time to focus and just write.

Hey God, Can We Talk?   Date:

Your mind should be clear. It's time to focus and just write.

Hey God, Can We Talk? ♡ Date:

Your mind should be clear. It's time to focus and just write.

Hey God, Can We Talk?   Date:

Your mind should be clear. It's time to focus and just write.

Hey God, Can We Talk? ♡Jesus   Date:

THE SCRIPTURE THAT KEPT ME ▶

WHAT CAN I DO DIFFERENTLY NEXT TIME?
▶
▶
▶

HOW CAN I REWARD MYSELF?
▶
▶
▶

WHAT WERE MY CHALLENGES? WAS I HARD ON MYSELF? DID I GIVE MYSELF GRACE? HAVE I FORGIVEN MYSELF? LET'S TALK TO GOD ABOUT IT!

HABIT BINGO

- You can either print this chart or draw your own. Add/remove habits based on what aligns with your personal goals.
- Set a Timeframe: Choose a timeframe for completing your Bingo (e.g., 30 days or a week). You can go at your own pace or aim to complete one habit per day.
- Mark Your Squares: Each time you complete a habit, mark off the corresponding square. You can use a sticker, check mark, or color in the box.
- Win Bingo: When you complete a full row, column, or diagonal, treat yourself with a reward! You can also keep playing until the whole chart is filled.

Wake Up Early	Exercise for 20 mins	Plan Your Day	Read for 15 minutes	Drink 8 Glasses of Water
Practice Gratitude	Write in a Journal	Take a 10-Minute Walk	Eat a Healthy Meal	Declutter for 10 Minutes
Practice Meditation	Call an accountability partner and update them on your goals	FREE SPACE	Learn Something New	Practice Self-Care
Get 7-8 Hours of Sleep	Organize Your Workspace	Work on a Hobby	Do a Random Act of Kindness	Reflect on Your Goals
Connect with Nature	Eat a Fruit or Vegetable	Complete a Task on Your To-Do List	Unplug for an Hour	Create a Budget

Step
workbook Eleven

Hey God, Help me with accountability.

Reflect on the role of community and accountability in your journey. Identify people or systems to help you stay on track.

LET'S CHECK IN

DATE _____

TOP 3 THINGS I WAS INTENTIONAL ABOUT
- _____
- _____
- _____

WHAT WERE MY PATTERNS?

THIS WEEK I FELT?

WHAT DO I NEED TO FOCUS ON NEXT?
_____
_____
_____
_____

WAS I TRIGGERED?

IN WHAT WAY WILL I SHOW UP FOR ME?

MY RANKING OF THE WEEK
☆ ☆ ☆ ☆ ☆

LET'S CREATE A PLAN

MONDAY | TUESDAY | WEDNESDAY

THURSDAY | FRIDAY | SATURDAY

APPOINTMENT TIMES | SUNDAY | TASK/REMINDERS

KEEP GOING!

Misc. doodle

TO-DO'S

PHOTO/reminders?

Just living my best life.

~ STEP 11 ~

HEY GOD, HELP ME WITH ACCOUNTABILITY.

Affirm - "I am open to constructive feedback and value the support of those who help me stay accountable to my goals."

Proverbs 27:17 NIV
"As iron sharpens iron, so one person sharpens another."

We need people! One of the hardest things for me was to accept the fact that I couldn't do life by myself. It took a nervous breakdown and almost admitting myself into a mental institution just to take a break. There were seasons in my life that were so difficult I didn't want to think, talk, or associate myself people. I fell into the trap of thinking: *"No one understands me... They haven't been through what I've been through... I don't need help; I can do it on my own... I'm the strong one – if I ask for help, they will judge me... Their problem is so much bigger than mine... They won't know how to give me the advice I need... I can't trust anyone with my struggles."*

These lies came from a place of fear, pride, or insecurity. I went a long time without any type of accountability because of the lies I told myself and I ended up breaking as a result of it. Depression and anxiety had me until I made the decision that I could no longer live my life that way anymore. Enough was enough. I asked God to give me some accountability partners and He over delivered. I joined a ministry called Chosen Wives. I'm now apart of a community who make me accountable so I won't wallow in the self-pity parties I would have by myself. I was able to encounter women who were able to help me through some of the most difficult times in my life. My accountability sisters were not just there to hear my problems but to go through life together. We would work on our physical goals, mental goals, financial goals, spiritual goals, social goals, marital plans and so forth. We would do meet up with the kids and pray for each other when we were experiencing something. We would show support towards each other in business ventures. If one had a problem, we would warfare and fast and pray with one another. We made sure that we would all be accountable to God.

Iron Sharpens Iron

Because I was able to make myself vulnerable with other women, it allowed me the opportunity to see the importance of having like-minded individuals to hold myself accountable to. My mental health has been so much better just because I stopped believing the lies. I started being intentional about placing myself in environments where I could be accountable to myself.

Just as iron sharpens iron through friction, people grow stronger, wiser, and more refined when they challenge, support, and hold each other accountable in love and truth. It encourages building meaningful connections that help you stay on the right path. Accountability is the very thing that encourages you to take responsibility for your actions, make intentional decisions, and stay aligned with the goals and values you have committed yourself to.

When I first started my process of being intentional to find accountability partners, it didn't always work out. In the early stages, I encountered another group of women who I felt were like-minded with similar business goals. We would meet up just to talk about what we had going on in our businesses and affirm each other consistently. It was a dream come true until it wasn't. I was so broken from the events that happened in the group that my guards went up. I lost faith and trust in people. The damage that was done left me so broken that I was going to give up on being vulnerable with others. Although what happened in that group hurt, I took it upon myself to take some time, regroup and try again. I say that to say this, finding people who you can connect with can be a difficult task. It can be even more difficult when you are guarded because of circumstances that were beyond your control, but don't give up just because of bad experiences.

People will disappoint you but don't allow that to distract you. You are on your pathway to heal and that includes being accountable to others. Sometimes, you will have to learn how to adapt and be vulnerable. Along my journey, I encountered many more groups of women who have stretched me in ways I didn't know I could. I'm so glad that I didn't give up on community.

Apart of my growth was creating this book and creating the community I needed throughout my journey. If you are reading this devotional, you are apart of it and for that, I thank you. I hope that you found this information helpful for your growth journey because I am accountable to you. Now it is your turn to be accountable to someone else.

Prayer:

Hey God, This accountability thing is hard. I have been hurt so many times in my past and have opened up myself more ways than I can count. New relationships don't seem promising to me. They put me in a position where I have to give myself to people and I'm not sure if I can. The trauma that I've experienced keeps me guarded but I want to let it down. I know that in order for me to become the version of myself that I need to be, it requires me to be vulnerable. It requires me to learn how to interact and be accountable for even the things I feel like I don't need people for. The truth is, I do need support. I need people who can be there for me and also people who I can show up for. I will disregard the lies that I tell myself and keep myself intentionally open to make new connections. In this process, I ask that you build my spirit of discernment and help me to recognize relationships that are mutually beneficial. I am open to constructive feedback and value the support of those who help me stay accountable to my goals.
In Jesus name!

Activity

Who do I call? (Accountability)

- Write down specific people you trust in each category.
- Schedule regular calls, texts, or meetings with these individuals to stay on track.
- Be Open: Share your goals and progress with honesty and allow them to provide feedback or encouragement.

Category	Why they can help?	Name
Creativity/Hobbies	Motivates you to pursue passions, develop talents, or stay consistent with hobbies.	
Spiritual Growth	Helps with prayer, Bible study, encouragement, faith and staying aligned with God's purpose.	
Career/Business	Provides advice, motivation, and accountability to stay on track with career goals or work projects.	
Health & Wellness	Encourages healthy habits, exercise, or staying consistent with self-care.	
Financial Goals	Offers accountability for budgeting, saving, and meeting financial milestones.	
Emotional Support	Listens without judgment and offers encouragement during emotional challenges.	
Relationships	Provides wisdom for navigating friendships, family, or romantic relationships.	
Personal Development	Encourages learning, skill-building, or achieving self-improvement goals.	

My Take-away's

1.
2.
3.
4.
5.

DEVOTIONAL NOTES

Top Three Affirmations

★ _____

★ _____

★ _____

Define your goals

▶ _____

▶ _____

▶ _____

▶ _____

▶ _____

▶ _____

▶ _____

▶ _____

▶ _____

▶ _____

▶ _____

▶ _____

Self Care Plans ✅ ❌

1. _____
2. _____
3. _____
4. _____
5. _____
6. _____

Prayer Focus ✅ ❌

1. _____
2. _____
3. _____
4. _____
5. _____
6. _____

Notes

BRAIN DUMP

DATE / /

Hey God, I'm busy a lot! Help me to be intentional.

CLEAR YOUR MIND!
What are all the things I can't stop thinking about?

HIGH PRIORITY
These are my non-negotiables, they have to get done!

LOW PRIORITY
These are important, but can wait.

FREE THOUGHTS
Remember to give yourself grace! You can't be everything to everyone. Fill up your cup and pour from the overflow.

5 Minutes of Meditation

S M T W TH F S

Breathe before writing

INHALE EXHALE INHALE EXHALE INHALE EXHALE

I'm intentionally meditating on?

* _____
* _____
* _____
* _____
* _____

Describe your feelings. You can draw or write.

My Action Step:
_____
_____

Expose meditation lies!

Sometimes, we think about things that are not true. Write down a truth to a lie you heard while meditating and confirm it with a scripture.

Example: I expose the lie that I'm not good enough because God says that I am fearfully and wonderfully made.

This Week's Highlight

Things that you overcame:
_____
_____
_____
_____

"This book of the law shall not depart out of thy mouth; but thou shalt meditate therein day and night." Joshua 1:8

Your mind should be clear. It's time to focus and just write.

Hey God, Can We Talk?   Date:

Your mind should be clear. It's time to focus and just write.

Hey God, Can We Talk? Date:

Your mind should be clear. It's time to focus and just write.

Hey God, Can We Talk?   Date:

Your mind should be clear. It's time to focus and just write.

Hey God, Can We Talk?   Date:

Your mind should be clear. It's time to focus and just write.

Hey God, Can We Talk? Date:

THE SCRIPTURE THAT KEPT ME ▶

WHAT CAN I DO DIFFERENTLY NEXT TIME?
▶
▶
▶

HOW CAN I REWARD MYSELF?
▶
▶
▶

WHAT WERE MY CHALLENGES? WAS I HARD ON MYSELF? DID I GIVE MYSELF GRACE? HAVE I FORGIVEN MYSELF? LET'S TALK TO GOD ABOUT IT!

MULTIPLE CHOICE

Accountability Quiz

1. *How do you typically respond when faced with a challenge?*

- A. Reflect
- B. Act
- C. Avoid
- D. Delay

2. *What motivates you most to stay accountable?*

- A. Goals
- B. Growth
- C. Fear
- D. Rewards

3. *What is the best way to track your progress?*

- A. Journals
- B. Apps
- C. Memory
- D. Conversations

4. *Who do you rely on for accountability?*

- A. Friends
- B. Family
- C. Mentors
- D. Myself

ANSWER KEY: 1.A, 2.A, 3.A, 4.C

Step workbook Twelve

Hey God, I am Empowered!

End your journey by stepping into confidence and empowerment. Celebrate your progress and commit to continuing your growth.

LET'S CHECK IN

DATE _____

TOP 3 THINGS I WAS INTENTIONAL ABOUT
- ○ _____
- ○ _____
- ○ _____

THIS WEEK I FELT?

WHAT WERE MY PATTERNS?

WHAT DO I NEED TO FOCUS ON NEXT?
_____
_____
_____
_____

WAS I TRIGGERED?

IN WHAT WAY WILL I SHOW UP FOR ME?

MY RANKING OF THE WEEK
☆ ☆ ☆ ☆ ☆

LET'S CREATE A PLAN

MONDAY | TUESDAY | WEDNESDAY

THURSDAY | FRIDAY | SATURDAY

APPOINTMENT TIMES | SUNDAY | TASK/REMINDERS

KEEP GOING!

Misc. doodle

TO-DO'S

PHOTO/reminders?

Just living my best life.

~ STEP 12 ~

HEY GOD, I AM EMPOWERED!

Affirm - "I have the courage to take bold steps toward my dreams."

Joshua 1:9 NIV
"Have I not commanded you? Be strong and courageous. Do not be afraid; do not be discouraged, for the Lord your God will be with you wherever you go."

Congratulations, you have made it towards the end of this devotional workbook. This may be the last section in this book but this is only the beginning of stepping out into the world as a much better version of yourself. Don't take for granted what you have accomplished so far. It took courage and boldness to be vulnerable in ways you hadn't before. I am grateful that you decided to embark on this community.

Embrace your power! The fact that you are reading this step means that you finished and are equipped for your journey. Don't be afraid to walk in the authority that has been given to you. Use the tools over and over again. If you feel like you need more, do this devotional again. Repeat some of the activities that helped you the most. Contact your accountability circle if you need to. Remember that empowerment is more than just feeling confident; it's about knowing that your strength comes from God.

In Joshua 1:9, God reminds Joshua—who was stepping into leadership after Moses—that courage and strength are not optional for the journey ahead. They are commands. But these commands come with a promise: "The Lord your God will be with you wherever you go." Like Joshua, you may face moments when the path before you feels overwhelming, your dreams feel distant, or fear creeps in. But God's word is assurance that you are never alone. His presence empowers you to step boldly into the unknown, make courageous decisions, and pursue the purpose He has set before you.

To be empowered is to believe that God's strength within you is greater than any obstacle ahead of you. You don't have to rely on your own abilities. You are empowered because the same God who commanded Joshua walks with you too. When you embrace this truth, fear loses its grip, and courage takes its place.

Hey God,

Thank You for reminding me that I am never alone. In moments of fear or uncertainty, help me remember Your promise to be with me wherever I go. Strengthen me to take bold steps toward the dreams and purpose You've placed in my heart. Fill me with Your courage and empower me to move forward with confidence.

In Jesus' name, Amen.

My Take-away's

1.
2.
3.
4.
5.

DEVOTIONAL NOTES

BRAIN DUMP

DATE / /

Hey God, I'm busy a lot! Help me to be intentional.

CLEAR YOUR MIND!
What are all the things I can't stop thinking about?

HIGH PRIORITY
These are my non-negotiables, they have to get done!

LOW PRIORITY
These are important, but can wait.

FREE THOUGHTS
Remember to give yourself grace! You can't be everything to everyone. Fill up your cup and pour from the overflow.

5 Minutes of Meditation

S M T W TH F S

Breathe before writing

INHALE EXHALE INHALE EXHALE INHALE EXHALE

I'm intentionally meditating on?

* _____
* _____
* _____
* _____
* _____

Describe your feelings. You can draw or write.

My Action Step:
_____
_____

Expose meditation lies!

Sometimes, we think about things that are not true. Write down a truth to a lie you heard while meditating and confirm it with a scripture.

Example: I expose the lie that I'm not good enough because God says that I am fearfully and wonderfully made.

This Week's Highlight

Things that you overcame:
_____
_____
_____
_____

"This book of the law shall not depart out of thy mouth; but thou shalt meditate therein day and night." Joshua 1:8

Your mind should be clear. It's time to focus and just write.

Hey God, Can We Talk?   Date:

Your mind should be clear. It's time to focus and just write.

Hey God, Can We Talk? Date:

Your mind should be clear. It's time to focus and just write.

Hey God, Can We Talk?   Date:

Your mind should be clear. It's time to focus and just write.

Hey God, Can We Talk? Date:

Your mind should be clear. It's time to focus and just write.

Hey God, Can We Talk?   Date:

THE SCRIPTURE THAT KEPT ME ▶

WHAT CAN I DO DIFFERENTLY NEXT TIME?
▶
▶
▶

HOW CAN I REWARD MYSELF?
▶
▶
▶

WHAT WERE MY CHALLENGES? WAS I HARD ON MYSELF? DID I GIVE MYSELF GRACE? HAVE I FORGIVEN MYSELF? LET'S TALK TO GOD ABOUT IT!

Final Step
workbook Bonus

Walking Boldly in Your Transformation!

~ BONUS WEEK ~

WALKING BOLDLY IN YOUR TRANSFORMATION

Affirm - I am equipped and empowered to live a life of purpose. God is with me in every step of my transformation.

Romans 12:2 NIV
"Do not conform to the pattern of this world, but be transformed by the renewing of your mind. Then you will be able to test and approve what God's will is—his good, pleasing and perfect will."

Transformation is going to feel strange. It might even feel like a place where you don't belong. It will feel like you are fighting and that the world is against you. You might even go back to, "Am I Enough?" I want to let you know that transformation is a process that doesn't end.

Every season of your life where elevation takes place will result in a new transformation. True transformation begins in the mind. Every thought, every choice, and every action you take contributes to the person you are becoming. Romans 12:2 is a reminder that true transformation requires a shift away from the patterns of the world and a deeper alignment with God's will. This isn't just about external changes—it's about renewing your thoughts and attitudes to reflect the mind of Christ as you elevate.

The key through the process is to have a level of self awareness so that you can prepare yourself to embrace the seasons you will face. As you journey, ask yourself: What thoughts, habits, or beliefs do I need to leave behind to walk fully in my transformation? Consider the ways you've already grown, and let that encourage you to keep moving forward. You can walk in boldness because you have been through and experienced the things and those seasons have equipped you. Walk boldly in it! There was a reason you suffered in pain.

One of my mentors, Dr. Tiffany Harris always says, "Who will lose, if you don't win!" I want your transformation to be a reminder that all of the hurts, pains and growth that you experienced was for the person that needed to win. Don't be surprised that others are and have been watching your transformation process. Some people stopped living their lives afraid because they have been watching you. You don't realize how many people you stopped from taking drugs, attempting to commit suicide, let go of that toxic abusive relationships etc. all because you have transformed. People are living a purposeful life because of you! God gave you a command, to walk with the courage and the strength that He has given you! It is time to walk boldly knowing that God has already equipped and prepared you for the road ahead.

Unapologetically MYSELF!

A Letter to Me

Write to your future self and set a date to read what you have written today. Reflect on where you are right now since starting this process. Celebrate your strengths and accomplishments. Affirm the person you are destined to be. Encourage yourself as you continue the journey and to keep showing up for yourself. Keep praying, reflecting, and taking small intentional steps forward. You are worthy of the life you're building.

Dear _____

everything will be OK

Proud of myself

Hey God,

Thank you for walking me through this process. Everyday hasn't been easy but each step revealed something in me that gave me the push to continue forward. You have given me the command that I am to walk with boldness and the courage you have given to me. I will do just that. You have given me the necessary tools to not be stuck and from this day forward there is no turning back. I will move with intention and walk in your purpose. I am all yours God.

In Jesus' name, Amen.

Scriptures to reflect on:

Psalm 139:14 - You are fearfully and wonderfully made.
Genesis 1:26 - We are the image of God.
Psalm 34:18 - The Lord is close to the brokenhearted.
Romans 12:2- Transformed by the renewing of your mind.
Jeremiah 29:11 - God's plans are good and give you hope.
Romans 8:1 - No Condemnation in Christ
Mark 9:23 - All things are possible when you believe.
Matthew 6:33 - Seek first the kingdom of God and His righteousness.
1 Corinthians 10:31 - Whatever you do, do it for the glory of God.

Recommended Song Playlist

In Spite of Me - Tasha Cobbs Leonard feat. Ciara
Gracefully Broken - Tasha Cobbs Leonard
AMEN AMEN- Sinmidele and Ore Macaulay
Press - Maranda Curtis
I'll Find You - LeCrae feat. Tori Kelly
Wanna Be Happy? - Kirk Franklin
On Time God - Woman Evolve Worship Feat. Chandler
I'll Just Say Yes - Brian Courtney Wilson
Nothing Else - Edward Rivera
The Blessing - Kari Jobe
Talitha Koum - Frankelle Outten
When I Pray - DOE
Life in the Party - Jennifer A Bryant

What's next...

Decide a time to spend in prayer and worship.
Listen to these songs or chose your own.
Reflect on the scriptures and what they mean to you.
Think about how God kept His promises with you.
Ask God to reveal things to you about you.
Talk to God, He wants to hear from you!

Notes from the author!

All of the information that you have read so far was a lot. I am so proud of you! Continue to talk and listen to God. Imagine how your life will change if only you dedicated fifteen minutes a day as a start and watch that increase.

My prayer is that you be intentional and take your time with your process. As you grow, you will fall in love with the version of yourself you are becoming. We are our best selves when we know who we are! Continue the journey, take breaks when needed but don't ever stop. You got this!

DON'T GIVE UP JUST BECAUSE THINGS ARE HARD

BE THE BEST VERSION OF YOURSELF

OLD WAYS WON'T OPEN NEW DOORS

YOU BECOME WHAT YOU BELIEVE

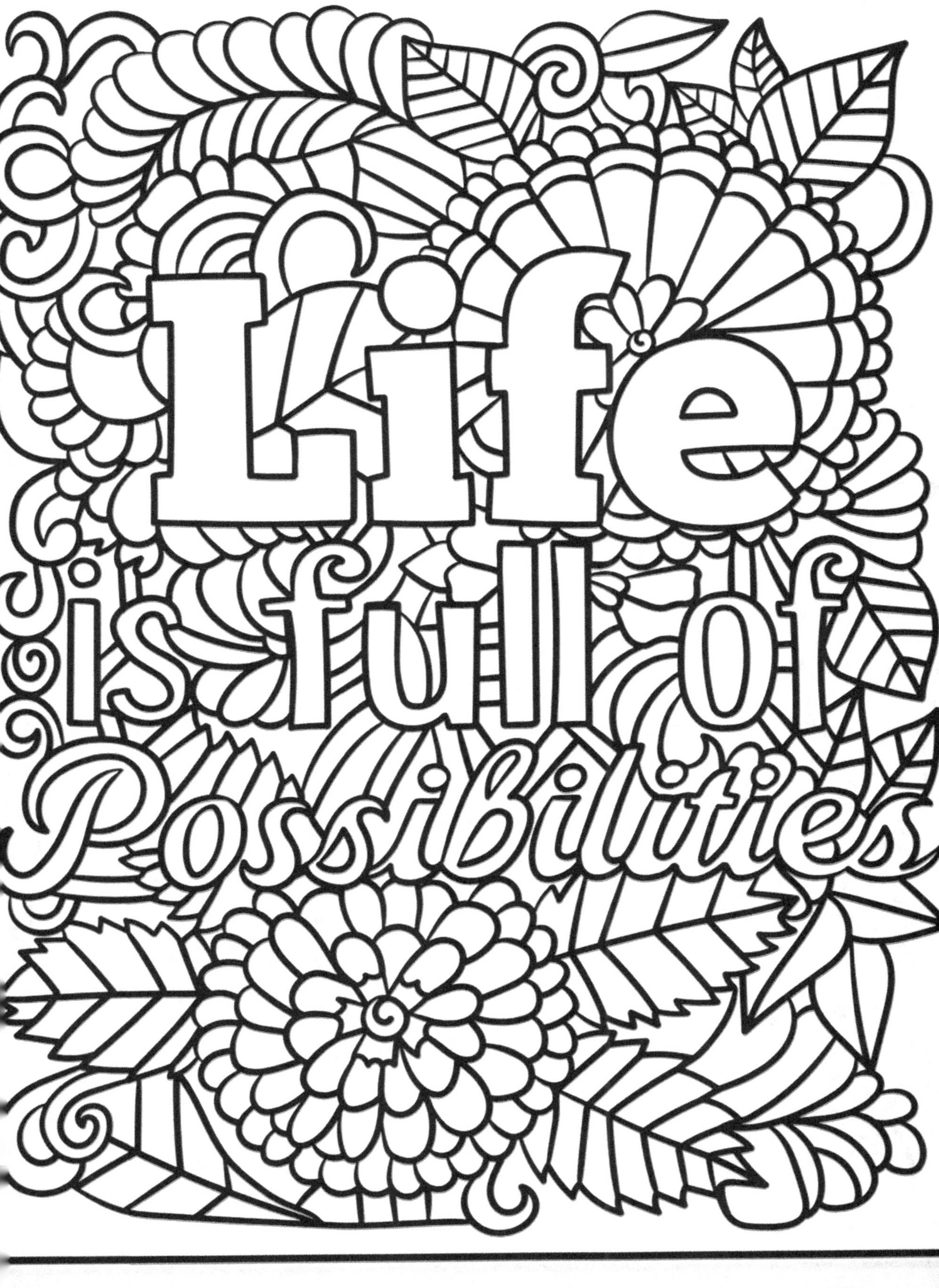
Life
is full of
Possibilities

Don't Stop until You're Proud

We all have a past and whether you're navigating the aftermath of sexual assault, emotional wounds, or seeking personal growth, each page encourages reflection, self-compassion, and personal breakthrough. This guide is perfect for those who want to be intentional on their journey. *"Hey God, Can We Talk,"* offers the tools you need to transform pain into power, brokenness into strength, and hopelessness into peace. Start your journey today and uncover the person you deserve to know by having more conversations with God.

Tammy is a Christian Sex Educator and an Intimacy and Relationship Coach. She teaches sexuality principles from a biblical perspective through her podcast, *"Sex for Saints,"* coaching sessions, workshops, books, and speaking engagements.

embrace the process

Made in the USA
Columbia, SC
28 April 2025